IT'S TIME TO TH...

GREATNESS
WITHIN

A FIVE-STEP FRAMEWORK TO STOP SEEKING VALIDATION AND CREATE A LIFE WORTHY OF YOU

BY JUAN R. ARROYO YAP

This work is based on my recollection of personal life events and the lessons I harvested from them. In some cases, I share concepts from my mentors and books I have read and give proper credit. If a correction needs to be made, I am happy to have the conversation.

Copyright © 2021 Juan R. Arroyo Yap

First paperback edition May 2021

ISBN 978-1-7371972-0-1 (eBook)
ISBN 978-1-7371972-1-8 (Paperback)

Cover design by me

Published by Juan on One Coaching, LLC
https://juanononecoaching.com

To everyone who has shared their life force with me and given me the opportunity to learn about myself and the world. Without a doubt, their contributions, however small, are part of the curriculum of my evolution.

CONTENTS

I Wasn't Meant to Write It but Needed to Be Written

I don't have a rags to riches story. I don't have an underdog background with the impressive movie-like success story.

What I have is a life with a comfortable living, a loving middle-class family and opportunities that allowed me to live 30 years of success that ended up being a life of lies.

Many say that if you don't have two or more books in you, don't even bother starting. Most people think that only the miracle stories and the extreme overcoming of obstacles are what people want to read and hear about.

Yes, it is always great to see the underdog succeed but that's not the general *way* of life.

I see that I spent 30 years living undercover. Thirty years of experiences, successes, failures, positive and negative emotions. Thirty years of seeing opportunities and experiencing the world. Thirty years of a life and career setup for success based on living someone else's life.

As I write this, I can't help but wonder if I have a book in me. Is it going to matter? *Is someone out there meant to read or listen to this story and get value from it?*

I wonder if I'm wasting my time and starting something that will never be finished like so many of the other things I have started before.

What I see as I watch my baby daughter grow is that we are born with a certain essence. A certain energy that seems unstoppable. It's a way of being that says to the universe, *"I am here and nothing can stop me. I am here to live. I am here to enjoy the experiences that may come. And, above all, I am here to use my life force to create a fun and loving journey for myself and others."*

- What happened to that life force as I grew up?
- What happened to all the confidence? To all the creative energy as I grew up and became an adult?
- Whatever happened to the need to explore, discover, and create new things just for leaving our mark on this world?

It's like I was recruited to be a secret agent and work undercover. To live in the shoes of a made-up character. One who follows certain rules and molds to his environment. And, who does things to gain the approval of some fictional group with the objective to be loved.

It's like I entered a much smaller world and forgot that love is who I am and what I came to this universe to give.

This is a story about how I took 30 years to discover I was living a lie and that my life hadn't even begun. *It's a story I think we all have to go through to start living OUR LIFE.*

This is how I remembered who I am. This is how I took five steps to start running my race, rediscover who I am, and restart the original mission I came to this world for...to explore, to create, and to love.

My friend, I don't have the absolute answers, I don't have the cookie cutter formula to give you what you want. But what I have is my journey to the starting line; steps that led me to find myself once more and begin the journey of living the life I am meant to live. It's the journey of my becoming.

May my steps help you begin transitioning out of your undercover life and help you get back on the path that reminds you of who you are so you can **go back to LIVING A LIFE WORTHY OF YOU.**

I think of these pages as the way back to my world, my voice, my standout way.

In peace,

~Juan

Chapter 1: It's Like I Was in a Movie

It's 4:45AM in the morning. I have been trying to calm down my 10-month-old baby since 4AM, so we can all sleep happily ever after. I finally managed to lay her down on the crib without waking her up and restart the process.

Silence...Everyone can go to sleep. Except, I'm too frustrated and riled up to do so. Instead, I reflect on life and meditate on what I am supposed to do. That's when this analogy begins.

I recall this memory of my teenage years.

I have just watched the movie *"The Green Mile"* with two high school friends.

As we discussed the movie, one of them asked, "What did you think? What message did you get out of it?

I immediately cried. It was a movie that fit me like a glove.

> *Side note: I thought it was just a movie, but I just realized it is a book by Stephen King. But I digress. Back to the story.*

The movie touched me, and to this day, is my favorite movie.

The movie felt like my life. I identified a lot with the character, John Coffey, portrayed by the late Michael Clarke Duncan.

If you have never watched the movie, John is a big black guy who was found carrying the bloodied body of a white girl. The movie is set in a racist white town and everyone around him thinks John is the killer.

When you first see John, you notice he is a massive human. He is around six-feet-five-inches, weighing about 350lbs of pure muscle. He looks so strong that he could probably break free from his handcuffs. But something looks off. Something is happening beyond his intimidating figure. It's his face and demeanor.

He looks in deep sorrow as if life has been taken out of him.

Was it because of the death sentence? Was it because everyone believed him to be guilty? Was it because he actually did it and got caught?

Everything initially points to him being guilty but the truth is not always in the appearance of things. Something about his energy said otherwise.

As the movie progresses, we realize John was simply a good guy that, while trying to help with his *gift,* was found at the wrong place, at the wrong time and life crumbled for him.

What I saw in John was a person committed to using his talents to help others but spent his entire life being misunderstood, devalued, repressed, and lonely.

He was a person with so much to give but totally worn down by the rules of the world and everyone else's expectations of him.

John had given up. He was at a point he didn't care what happened to him. He just wanted peace. He wanted a place to belong. A place where he could be himself and allow his light to shine freely.

The movie plays along and grants John his wish. He found a few who believed in him. He turned most of his security detail to his side. And, even though his sentence wasn't lifted, he finds peace.

Evidently, I'm only sharing how I perceived this movie and the parts that touched my soul.

That is how I felt back in high school. I felt misunderstood and out of place. I believed I had a lot to give. I had this strong passion to serve others, but I felt like no one was listening. I felt like I was doing everything wrong. I just couldn't figure out how to make myself heard. I was stuck in a nightmare.

Fortunately, I didn't die like John. I did find a few who believed in me. I evolved and learned to focus on the things I could control.

But truth be told, fifteen years later, at 30, I faced my metaphorical death sentence. I hit my emotional and mental bottom. I wanted to give up.

The Moment I Realized I Have Been Living A Lie

It's May of 2012. I have been very busy at work with the usual 80-hour work weeks. I'm sitting in front of the computer analyzing financial projections, and minding my business, when my boss at the time (I'll call him Blessing), stands by the office door and says, *"can I see you in my office?"*

If you are human, you know the feeling. *"That cannot be good"*, I thought for a few seconds before thinking about how much I had to get done and I didn't have time for a one-on-one.

As I walked in and sat down. *Blessing* looked at me, maybe a little anxious, and said, *"I cannot do this anymore, you have three months to find something else."*

I immediately exploded and said "Who the f*** do you think you are? You are tired of this? I'm the one who's tired of your stupid nonsense and the lack of respect I get even though I know more about the job than you do!"

Relax...I didn't say it out loud. It was all in my head. Whether I was right or wrong didn't matter. I was told to pack my things and go. Even though, several months earlier, *Blessing* told me he needed my help.

Now, I had to find something else.

I didn't. I was too busy to think about finding another job. I had government deadlines to meet, a team to manage, and a group of regional VPs that needed my help with running their business.

Fortunately, in August of 2012, as the directors discussed talent performance, someone gave me a chance to be in a different role within the same department working 40 hours a week instead of the usual 80.

Similar to John Coffey's story, I faced a death sentence (losing my prior job); I found someone who believed in me (gave me a new job); but I didn't have peace.

The additional 40 hours of *free* time a week gave me time to think and reflect on what had happened.

While I had a job, I found myself confused and frustrated but I couldn't explain why.

The frustration grew into a version of depression and life crisis.

One afternoon, I found myself in the corner of the office break room, staring out a window on the 20th floor.

If you would have walked in, you would have noticed nothing wrong until you got a few feet away from my face.

That day, I was alone and felt as lonely as anyone could feel. I was feeling like a failure and believed life would never get better.

I have had success. In less than eight years, I had gone from entry level to managing a team responsible for pricing a block of business generating $1.2B in revenue. All of it before the age of 30. I had a comfortable life. *And yet, I felt lost and like giving up.*

In retrospect, that's the day I realized John Coffey's situation had repeated in my life. Fifteen years after watching the movie, I was still living a life in hiding.

While I have had success up to that day, I felt out of place. Despite all the efforts to improve my communication skills, the many ways I have helped others, and the hundreds of people I had worked with, I still felt misunderstood, powerless and out of place.

I felt like something was wrong but couldn't place my finger on it; so, I sat down to journal.

I grabbed a notepad and at the top of the page I wrote, "What happened? How did I get here? What am I going to do now?" As soon as I finished writing the series of questions, three vivid memories came to mind.

Memory #1 - The Dad Moment

First, I saw myself as 11 years old. My father is walking beside me. We are on a baseball field walking towards center field. The outfield fence is a line of trees followed by what looks like a basketball court and playground. Just before the trees is a bunch of kids and one adult.

It turns out we are there because it's the first day of league play and we are meeting this person to see if I can play.

I had never played baseball. My dad always wanted me to be active with some exercise. I had tried karate, basketball, soccer, and today, it was the turn for baseball.

Little did I know that day would be the first day of a nine-year long baseball journey.

I turned out to have talent for the game. And being left-handed I was *special*. With a little practice and dedication, I represented Panama in the 1994 Latin American Little League Tournament. For the next nine years, I played baseball almost every day.

It was a career where I represented my country twice, and led to receiving an offer to play professionally for what used to be the Montreal Expos (now the Washington Nationals).

I didn't know what I was doing. I was just going with the flow and following a habit that started with a little push from my dad.

Memory #2 - A Moment With Mom

After remembering my success with baseball, I saw myself on the passenger's seat of my mom's car. It's a white BMW and we were driving down one of the main avenues of Panama City. We were headed home.

We stopped at the intersection. As I'm people watching, she turned to me and asked, *"It's your senior year in high school, what are you planning to study in college?"*

I didn't know so I shrugged and said, "I don't know, probably one of the engineering tracks."

The car moved again and, about 30 seconds later, my mom says, "Some actuaries I know say that, because you are good at math, you should study actuarial science."

I thought that sounded different and, since I wanted to be different, I agreed to it.

It was an interesting decision to make because it wasn't an available degree in Panama. It required me to leave the country. Mom wanted me to learn English so I applied to schools in the U.S.A.

Four years later, I finished school with a double major in actuarial science and statistics, and a double minor in Psychology and Business.

Once again, I just went with the flow and succeeded.

Which brings us to the third memory.

Memory #3 - The Ladder of Success
Armed with my degree, I found a job in the USA to improve my English and gain experience before returning to Panama.

I'm 21 years old and ready to make a difference and use what I learned in school.

It took a few months, but, in the end, I found a job at a health insurance company as an overpaid copy maker. That wasn't my title but it's what I did.

I spent most of my days fixing the printer, making copies, collating documents and taking them to be signed by the VIPs.

It was busy work but I felt great because I was finally part of the workforce.

I got in early and left late. I followed orders. I suggested improvements. I helped wherever and whenever I could. I met or exceeded expectations.

I repeated that enough times and, soon enough, I got promoted. In a couple years, I was managing a small region. In less than five years, I was in charge of three regions. By the 7th year, I was managing a division generating $1.2B in revenue.

I was making $104,000 a year.

Success once more...all by going with the flow.

But it all came crumbling down...which brought me back to the office's break room.

The Decision

As I brought my presence back to the office's break room, I wondered, *"why did I remember those three memories?"* Memories I had long forgotten. And then, it hit me.

ALL THE SUCCESSES HAVE BEEN DRIVEN BY ME GOING WITH THE FLOW OF WHAT OTHER PEOPLE SAID I SHOULD DO!

In that moment, I realized most of my life I had been following someone else's image of who I needed to be to succeed. I succeeded and failed. Which begged the question, *"If I can follow best practices and fail, why not just follow what I want to do and see what happens?"*

Right then and there, I decided if I would ever fail again, I might as well do it following what I wanted to do.

Getting Fired Once More

That decision was the beginning of transitioning from living undercover, and trying to succeed by following other people's expectations, to creating a life that is an extension of who I am and who I am becoming. A journey to creating a life worthy of me; and the experiences, the content for this book.

> *"The content of your life is the curriculum*
> *of your evolution."*
>
> *~Mary Morrissey*

What ensued for the next six years was a process of unlearning, discovering, testing and relearning to rediscover who I am.

In 2018, six years after discovering I had been living a lie, my manager and I had a one-on-one meeting.

I recall passing by the executive assistant and seeing her nod at me like saying, *"be ready..."*

I walked in expecting bad news.

My manager was standing behind his desk waiting for me. As I walked in, he said something similar to, "I have Jenny News on the line, an HR consultant. She's on the phone because, today,

I'm letting you know your position is going to be eliminated 60 days from today."

I laughed and quickly said *"awesome!"*

What was a devastating conversation in 2012 was now a relief. For whatever reason, I was happy and relieved to hear the news.

I was relieved for a couple reasons.

1. **Validation:** Two months prior, after being reprimanded by HR for something I said and someone else took out of context, I heard my internal voice say, *"You have to leave this company."* I didn't do it but now the universe was deciding for me.
2. **Results:** I had invested the time, money, and effort to pursue my passion and had successfully connected with a group of people that valued what I brought to the table via blogs, personal development forums, and weekly leadership discussions.

Today, I recognize few people are glad to be fired twice by the same department but it was confirmation I wasn't valued and it was time to move on.

I had no idea of the challenges that would come later, but at that moment, I was certain it was time for something new.

The rest of the conversation with my manager is irrelevant. I recall being told I could take the rest of the day off but I stayed. I went back to the famous break room and kept doing my work like any day prior.

In hindsight, I am thankful for a friend who warned me, a few weeks in advance, of the possibility of me getting fired. It marked the beginning of a new phase and possibly the push to write this book.

This Book's Purpose: Five Steps to Stop Seeking Validation & Start Thriving Your Way

What I seek to do with this book is twofold. Firstly, I'm writing to process the events of my life and find my authentic voice. Secondly, I'm sharing the lessons from my journey with the objective to help you design your framework to create a life worthy of you.

This is about showing a path you can use to design a life where you feel free to be yourself rather than being in a constant struggle to fit in and seek acceptance or validation.

As I have lived through the five steps, I acknowledge the constant struggle between creating my path and forcing myself to fit in someone else's description of what life should be.

I won't pretend to have all the answers but I share my journey as an example of what could come if you decide to create a life worthy of you.

Your mission, if you choose to accept it, is to simply engage with the process, give it an honest consideration, and put it to the test while you develop your framework through which you make life decisions.

In going from being fired and feeling like a failure to being fired and happy about it, I lived through five stages that can be grouped into five steps. I call them the Greatness Within Framework.

1. Passionately **Challenge** Everything You Know

2. Courageously **Discover** Your Light
3. Purposely **Claim** Your Space
4. Confidently **Filter** Your Critics
5. Gratefully **Welcome** The Journey

Here's a brief description of the framework:

Step #1 - Passionately Challenge

Recall how I mentioned feeling like I was living undercover. I was trying to succeed by following the rules that applied to this persona.

As I answered the question, "Who really am I if I have been living under someone else's idea of who I should be?"

I concluded that my first step was to validate everything I thought described me. I had to challenge everything I thought I was.

Step #2 - Courageously Discover

This is the part that many people, myself included, easily forget. For decades, I got so busy trying to meet people's expectations and pursue the "safe" job that I lost myself in the details. I forgot what it means to learn, discover, and create. I forgot who I was.

This step is about letting go of inhibitions and taking the time to remember who we are and what we can do. It's about stepping into the unknown to find our essence: the good, the bad, the ugly, and the great.

Step #3 - Purposely Claim

I spent three decades going with the flow to realize that, while life was good, I was still following society's agenda.

Purposely claiming your space is about acting with a specific intention in mind that's tied to who you are and where you are trying to go. It's about making yourself known.

Step #4 - Confidently Filter

This is my daily battle. Not a day goes by without me having to listen to myself or someone else contradict what I am trying to create.

Everyone wants to give their *two cents* to protect me from pain.

This step is about learning whose voice to listen to and what are the options to overcome the roadblocks that show up along the way.

Step #5 - Gratefully Welcome

This is my crux. I can be so focused on getting things right that I forget the journey of my becoming is not meant to be a perfect straight line.

Since 2012, I have had to learn to be present and enjoy the many ways the Universe participates in creating the life I desire. It has been the hardest thing for me to do but a blessing I cannot deny.

This step is about learning to be open and present to the unexpected ways the life we want comes to fruition.

Regardless of where you are in your journey, the Greatness Within Framework seeks to provide just enough a foundation to get you started while still allowing you to discover your way of getting it done.

Chapter 2: Three Signs That You May Be Living a Lie

Before expanding on each of the steps of the framework, I share some signs I missed that were an indication of living in the constant pursuit of validation.

It's interesting to reflect on the decades before the break room epiphany because, up until that point, I truly believed I was independently pursuing my goals. I didn't realize that I was functioning under the constraints set by my upbringing and surroundings.

There's nothing wrong with this approach when we are young and don't know any better.

I was raised the best way my parents could, and I absorbed the rest from the circumstances and people I interacted with because I believed others had the answers.

Yes, there's a place for external feedback but, often, other people's experiences don't necessarily apply to us.

Nevertheless, here's what I noticed in hindsight.

Sign #1 - The First Role Models

Like any human, I came to this world with only two fears: the fear of loud noises and the fear of sudden changes in height. Everything else I learned along the way.

My baseball story and how I chose which college degree are just two of the many choices I made in order to please my parents. Remember, I thought they knew better; and in many life subjects, they did.

One of the clearest examples of me copying someone else's lifestyle is how I interact with others. I grew up seeing my dad telling his truth, being brutally honest, and trying to do the right thing. My dad was also focused on doing things the right way.

Thus, it shouldn't be a surprise that I spent my entire life being quick to tell people what I thought about a situation and their actions. It's very easy for me to share my opinion and be confident in how I say it.

From my mom, I mimicked being friendly and caring about others. This is a contrast to what I learned from my dad.

Ultimately, I listened to both and followed their advice to honor what they had done for me and to, unconsciously, earn their approval.

It was a very instinctual behavior to observe the people and environment I was in to figure out what I needed to do to find my place and belong.

Like someone going undercover to learn the target's preferences, mannerism, language, mode of operations, and thinking process, I did the same thing as I grew up.

Have you noticed something similar in your life?

How well has it worked for you?

I'm not saying this is right or wrong, and I'm not criticizing my parents either. I'm simply pointing out that *mimicking someone else is bound to create the life of the one we mimic, not the one we are meant to live.*

Maybe, the question needed to be answered here is "**Is the life I am mimicking the life that I desire?**"

Sign #2 - Living Like The Experts Say

I have noticed that, in certain situations, I pay too much attention to what other people say I should do. I have this perception that if I say or do things too different from what others are doing, I will look like I'm crazy.

> *Side note: If you think this last statement contradicts my earlier statement about not being afraid to say what I think, you are correct.*
>
> *There are circumstances where my perfectionism supersedes my straight talk. It is not that I don't say what I think but that I dilute the message to increase the chances of my idea being accepted. It's a variation of people pleasing, which I discuss later in the book.*

There is a benefit to having mentors, study books, and attend trainings and seminars. But when the focus is all about consuming and applying what experts say, when will there be the opportunity to develop inner strength and instincts.

When my personal development journey started, I spent years consuming all types of resources but rarely took time to identify what applied to me and what didn't. I simply took the concepts and assumed they were true and forced myself to use them.

It can all be summarized into lack of self-confidence. It's the evolution of me as a child looking up to my parents for what's needed to survive.

This behavior is identified when our first reaction before a decision is made is to wonder what parents, research, friends, family, and any other external source of information says on the matter.

- What do you think?
- Let me check with...
- Everyone is telling me to...
- Dr. Jenny says I should...
- This person I follow says to...

Again, there is a time and place for external counsel but *when all personal decisions are made after consuming someone else's ideas, how can I be so sure I'm actually living my life?*

Sign #3 – Not Wanting to Offend or Bother

This is a variation of avoidance of conflict. It's a tendency to avoid creating any perceived negative consequences from someone's actions or words.

This shows up in my life in the way I love to help others but don't like to ask for help because it can be troublesome for the other person. It also shows up when I am careful with my words and mannerisms to avoid others getting defensive.

Due to negative past experiences, I have seen myself change behaviors and carefully pick my words and the topics I engaged with to blend in and prevent offending someone.

It is like I act at 60%-70% of my intensity to avoid appearing intimidating.

For example, I recall saying *"I'd like to lead but from the back."*

I used to say it because I could avoid offending someone with my words or actions.

I would modify my behaviors to create a persona that would fit the mold of what the people around me expected me to be.

The adaptation was subtle but it was present.

As I understand it, I internalized the change as part of my personality to not want to bother others with my requests, ideas, or behaviors.

To this day, I still place other people's comfortability before my own. It's my version of being a people pleaser. I share more on this in the *Purposely Claiming Your Space* chapter.

Putting It All Together

What helps me simplify the process of identifying if I am living a lie or not is taking time to reflect and ask these three questions:

1. To what extent is my life being ruled by what I think my parents want of me?
2. How quick am I to accept and apply expert advice to my life without actually validating that it works for me?
3. How often do I change my actions and words to fit in with the crowd I am hanging out with?

This is not about ignoring everything other people say but taking the time to evaluate what applies and what works best for where I am trying to go and who I want to become.

There is also no right or wrong answer to these questions. It is not an exam. The point is to become aware of the extent other people's beliefs drive what we say or do.

Choose: The Blue Pill or The Red Pill?

In this classic scene from the movie *The Matrix*, Morpheus offers Neo the choice to know the truth.

If you haven't seen the movie, I'm sharing an excerpt transcript of the conversation.

> *Morpheus: The matrix is everywhere. It is all around us. Even now in this very room. You can see it when you look out your window or when you turn on your television. You can feel it when you go to work, when you go to church, when you pay your taxes.* **It is the world that has been pulled over your eyes, to blind you from the truth.**
>
> *Neo: What truth?*
>
> *Morpheus: That you are a slave Neo. Like everyone else you were born into bondage, born into a prison that you cannot smell or taste or touch. A prison for your mind. Unfortunately, no one can be told what the matrix is. You have to see it for yourself.* **This is your last chance. After this, there is no turning back. You take the BLUE pill...the story ends...you wake up in your bed and believe whatever you want to believe. You take the red pill...you stay in wonderland...and I'll show you how deep the rabbit hole goes.**

Neo: (reaches out for the red pill and right before he grabs it...)

Morpheus: Remember, all I'm offering is the truth, nothing more.

Whenever I'm helping someone determine what they want from life, this choice always comes up. Sooner or later, the person reaches a crossroad where the choice is to continue living life as a character in a movie or start discovering the truth of who they are. Many, including myself, succumb to the pressure of such a decision.

On one hand, life in the matrix is ordered by rules and the system. If I follow the rules, everything is fine. Similarly, living life by following other people's expectations and advice is very convenient. Choosing the blue pill and going with whatever society expects appears to be the path of least resistance to me.

On the other hand, choosing the red pill means traveling to unknown destinations with only the promise of finding my truth. But I have to ask, *"what is truth? I have been living this life for so many years...is there really something else? I mean, I feel like something is off but I don't really know whether it is worth it to leave this life in order to find my truth."*

Here's an exercise to make the options more practical.

In order to engage with this process, I suggest you submit yourself to the narrative: see and feel yourself there.

Option 1: The Blue Pill
Suppose you live life as you are doing it right now for the next 10 years.

- Same habits and activities,
- Same friends,

- Similar job, and
- Similar environment

You are now 10 years older, saved money, achieved success, but life is pretty much the same.

- How fulfilled and satisfied are you with this life 10 years later?
- Are there unanswered questions?
- Is there frustration? Remorse?
- Feels like something is missing?
- Any personal goals placed on hold or forgotten?

What's nice about this path is that you have already done it. You know what is coming and how to do well at it. You know the mechanics and are confident things will work the same way as they have.

If this future has you excited, then maybe for you it is totally okay to keep going the way you are right now.

Option 2: The Red Pill
Now, imagine making a different choice.

For the next 10 years, you take small steps towards getting to know yourself, identifying what you want from life, and stepping confidently into unknown territory with the freedom to pursue what you love.

- You take five minutes per day to imagine a 10 out of 10 life.
- You allow yourself to consider what's beyond the paycheck and how amazing it feels to improve the lives of those around you.

- You brainstorm what is an ideal career for you.
- You picture yourself proud and fulfilled after a day's work.

You take these tiny steps regularly until, one day, you find yourself with a completely different life.

These are 10 years of intentional daily steps to create a meaningful and fulfilling life.

But there's a catch...it's unknown territory.

You haven't seen this place before. It's a side of you that you didn't know existed. It's a new challenge. It's a new path that may contain obstacles you have never faced. The people around you may not want to be a part of it. You may need to make new friends, learn new things, and work hard to make it work.

Does it still sound exciting? Are the results from self-awareness, confidence, and freedom worth it to go through unknown territory?

It's decision time. You have to choose.

- You can pick the blue pill and continue to live your life trying to meet everyone else's expectations of you while being aware something is missing. Or,
- You can pick the red pill and start a journey that has the potential to clarify who you are, what you want from life, gain the confidence to step into it, and the freedom to pursue your passions without caring about what other people think of you and the journey.

I cannot choose for you just as no one could have chosen for me back in 2012.

I recall how I felt when I learned of the fallacy of my life. I had been preaching about being myself and pursuing my journey when, in reality, I had allowed the need to belong and make my parents proud dictate my activities.

I felt dumb and stupid but I also found an opportunity to give myself permission to shine and enter a new adventure. It was a freeing feeling because I was now aware other people don't know what's best for me. I had failed following their advice, so I might as well learn to listen to my inner voice and attempt building a life according to my passions, values, and dreams.

This is where the adventure begins.

If you continue on, these chapters share the tools I used to get started and address the obstacles that showed up along the way. I grouped these tools into the five steps I briefly explained earlier in the chapter.

I look forward to sharing the journey with you.

Chapter 3: Screw Playing The Hand You Were Given

Welcomed. I am assuming you reached this point because you chose the red pill.

If I had to summarize the previous chapters in a sentence, I'd quote the words attributed to comedian Jim Carrey,

> *I think everybody should get rich and famous and do everything they ever dreamed of so they can see that it's not the answer."*
>
> ~*Jim Carrey*

I take a moment to share how Jim's statement relates to my prior life and the *Greatness Within Framework.*

Recall the three memories I shared. The driving force or need behind my actions was to find a place to belong. For decades, society and parental expectations created an environment in which the concept of self-worth was anchored in having more and getting accepted by those around me.

More…

- accolades

- degrees
- years of experience
- membership to private groups
- awards
- finest behaviors
- cars and house
- wearing branded clothing
- etc.

I was sold the idea that becoming who I am meant to be is achieved by following a certain formula of appearances and success.

If such approach was the appropriate one, don't you think there wouldn't be rich people committing suicide?

Why would a person with $10 million in the bank continue to want more money?

I don't think it's because of greed. While there are greedy individuals, the constant thirst for more is a misappropriation of our human nature.

Just like I continued to seek for more ways to make more friends, more money, improve my reputation, get more people to listen to what I had to say, and build fame, the millionaire continues to seek for more.

Why?

I submit my experience as an explanation.

There's a part of me that knows that the greatness of an individual doesn't come from the acquisition of external riches but the full expression of the talents and power that resides within the individual. In addition, a part of me knows that the only way to recognize I am complete is to allow my internal wisdom to direct the course of my life.

Now, by this I don't mean we won't need help or to acquire things. It simply means that self-worth comes from within the individual and our lives possessions and circumstances should reflect that internal belief.

The lie the world wants me to believe is that for me to be happy, I need to pursue what the world considers successful and valuable.

Today, I am not surprised I was depressed for being fired in 2012. It wasn't the fact of losing the job but the realization that, for 30 years, I had been saying "No" to myself and allowing others to define and mold who I "needed to be."

Sounds familiar? Have you sensed something is off but continue to search for what it might be by meeting other people's expectations of you?

If you do, I know the feeling. If you haven't, that's okay, too.

I recall the moment I realized I had been living a lie. I didn't know where to begin. All I knew to do was to go back to what I knew to do best: *challenge the status quo.*

Thus, *the first step of the Greatness Within Framework was born: passionately challenge everything you think you know about who you are so you can make room for what truly represents you.*

When Life Is Just A Deck of Cards

Many people, myself included, reinforce the idea of learning to play the hand they are dealt but it never occurs to them that they can ask for a new hand.

I chose to do the latter.

I visualized taking a deck of cards and writing down on each card something I knew or believed about myself. Then, I threw all the cards on the table and only picked the cards that resonated with me.

Let me stop right here and invite you to visualize this analogy as a way to set up the stage for what's next.

Take a slow deep breath in while allowing your mind to slow down. Feel your body relax and focus on your breathing. Now, exhale slowly and let any stress, deadlines, and to-dos go with it. Keep breathing slowly as you engage in this visual.

Suppose you are exploring your life. You may be questioning the meaning of life. You may be trying to redefine yourself. Or, you may be attempting to learn more about yourself.

You take a deck of cards and remove the cards from their case. You then take one card at a time and write something on each card that represents who you are.

Each card has something that you identify with and it's something you would use to answer the question "Who are you?"

When finished, you pick the cards back up and order them. This deck of cards represents everything that defines you.

Now, take the deck and throw it towards a table several feet away.

As you see the cards fly away and make a mess, you are seeing everything that defines you go with it. You are letting it all go and trying to start over.

Everything you are is gone.

Some cards fall on the floor. Some cards fall on the table. Some are face down, others are face up. Some are stuck under table legs, and so forth.

How are you feeling as you look at the mess?

The question I had to answer before "asking for a new hand" was **what would happen to my identity if I threw away all that defined me?**

When I started the journey of asking for a new hand or picking only the cards that resonated with me, I struggled.

I visualized the mess and felt the urge to do a few things...

- I saw the cards stuck under the table and cabinets and wanted to pick them back up.
- I saw the dirty floor and felt the need to quickly clean up the cards and put them on the table
- I then saw the face down cards and needed to flip them over and appreciate their colors.
- Once I got them all cleaned, I "had" to put them in order, stack them, and place them back in the box.

I would justify picking all the cards back up with phrases like:

- ...but I really like this one
- ...this one is the one my father said I should do
- ...my friends like this one a lot
- ...this one makes me feel important

- ...and, I have always done it this way

This analogy might be silly but it sure fits what happened to me. I let go of the things I identified with and immediately looked for ways to justify keeping them.

I speculate you will face similar doubts and urges as you go through this exercise. I suggest finding a way to give yourself permission to engage in the process and allow the learning journey to show you what is yours.

It may cause anxiety to temporarily remove your identity vestments and start anew. The mind will immediately fight to keep everything in place. In those moments, it is valuable to remember this challenging process is happening because what has been done is not working.

Once I was willing to let it all go and embrace the temporary emptiness, I was able to objectively act.

Here's what I discovered as I virtually observed all the cards spread across the table.

There are four (4) core groups of things that need to be challenged:

1. What I own
2. What I look like
3. What I do
4. What I think

As you read these categories they may not make as much sense as you think. Or, they may sound like common sense. But, remember, this is about unlearning everything you think you know about yourself. This is an exercise to redefine your identity. How often do you use those four categories to answer the question *"Tell me about who you are?"*

I share my thoughts on the matter and what I did before you decide whether to continue this journey or not. Unlike *"The Matrix,"* nothing is stopping you from going back and picking up the blue pill.

#1 - I Am Not My Possessions

This category is really about status and the labels that come with our possessions. It is very interesting to notice how much power we give to the things we own. Our clothing, the house we live in, the neighborhood, the school we went to, the circles of friends we have, the groups we belong to, jobs we have, etc.

This is all about using external things that formed the concept of our identity.

To use a taboo subject as an example, I'll use *religious association*.

What type of person is a Buddhist, a Catholic, a Muslim, a Sikh, a Baptist, or an Atheist?

Do you have any specific preconception of what type of person **should** someone be if they belong to a specific religion?

Let's use more common labels: banker, consultant, teacher, mother, vice president, actuary, economist, digital marketer, lawyer, author, salesperson, stripper, housemaid, etc.

What I have found is that it is easy to use the title to define who we are and we are quick to adapt our behaviors and thinking to what we believe the labels represent. We continue this behavior until we identify with it. And so, the role playing begins.

Have you ever met a person that gets fired from their precious job and enters a depression when they cannot seem to find the same job in a different company? How about someone who wants to switch companies but refuses to take a pay cut because *"they know they are worth so much more."*

I have used this thinking myself.

I recall deciding to stop taking actuarial exams. I was considered an Associate Actuary. It didn't take long to see my peers, who took exams at a similar time, get promoted much faster for the simple fact they kept taking exams. We had the same job. But they made more money and were promoted just because they had passed more exams.

I find nothing wrong with that approach because I recognize my peers had put more effort in finishing the actuarial exams track.

As I saw them get promoted, I doubted my worth because I was "stuck" with an Associate Actuary title. I doubted my decision. I doubted myself. I doubted that I could add any value to the company.

A few years later, I was promoted to the same level as my peers in recognition of my contributions to the company. I had a six-figure salary and many came to me for mentoring. It took a little longer than others but this promotion helped me see that the title didn't change who I was and the impact of my contributions.

What was more eye-opening was that my title didn't change. I had the same Associate Actuary title but I had the same compensation as someone a couple levels higher.

This disconnect between title and contribution value was difficult to see at the moment but, in hindsight, **it helped me** internalize the value I bring to the world comes from something more than the things I own, the titles earned and the circles of people we are a part of.

The sobering question to ponder here is: *Who are you if I stripped you from everything you currently own?*

If the answer is "nothing," I understand. And, I'd suggest that even in such a dire situation there is still a chance to be of value because you are alive and have the choice to get up and create something new.

If there are doubts about my last statement, I only have to point to Nelson Mandela, who spent 27 years in prison, removed from everything he owned, and still went to become a worldwide unanimously recognized symbol of leadership and changed the course of a nation.

Self-worth doesn't come from the things we have. It's something that comes from within us.

#2 - I Am Not My Looks

Back in 2005 when I purchased my first car, I went to visit a local Toyota dealer. I was wearing an old pair of shorts and a T-shirt. I was walking through the lot checking out the different cars. After 10 minutes, a salesperson came out with a grumpy look on his face to ask me what I was there for and if I needed help.

I was a little shy when I asked him for the best deal on the 2006 Toyota Corolla model. He looked at me dismissively and said "we don't do deals here..." and walked off.

I guess he didn't know that I had enough cash in the bank to buy two cars and I was making more money than most people walking into the parking lot that day.

I didn't give it much thought back then but it would have been easy for me to think there was something wrong with me. I had allowed those interactions to affect me in the past.

It's a natural thing for us to want respect and to be accepted regardless of our clothing style and physical appearance.

Yet, we are quick to "dress up" when going to a job interview, a bank, church, weddings, business seminars, etc. We do it because we think the "look" will show how important we are to the world or because we want to feel we belong.

- If a person is missing a limb, would you say they are no longer a person?
- Can a person with an uncommon physical appearance add value to the world?
- Is it possible for someone who looks homeless to share some of life's wisdom?

What's most valuable about breaking the connection of physical appearance from the identity of a person is that our bodies can change but we may not change with it.

There's not much to think about it. We can gain or lose weight. Our skin can change colors. We can modify our body. We get older. And yet, after all of it, we are still the same person.

Our carcass can change but the power within is still the same.

As some experts like to say, our body is simply the vehicle that takes us from one place to another. It's the medium through which we can interact with the world around us.

#3 - I Am Not My Behaviors

I could be a professional people watcher. I enjoy watching others go about their day and try to figure out what they are thinking, what's their intention behind their actions, and what type of person they are.

I am quick to use behavior to guesstimate the personality. While there can be a correlation between a person's behavior and their identity, that's not the absolute truth.

Just as physical appearance can change, so can behaviors. Just because I am lazy today, doesn't mean I am not capable of being disciplined and have infinite energy to pursue something I'm passionate about.

I can speak into this lazy vs passionate contrast by using my experience in a leadership training trip I participated in called *"Transformation Paraguay"*.

This was a four-day trip to teach government officials, business leaders, and successful professionals how to use values as a framework to develop a leadership culture. During the four-day trip I slept about 12 hours but I never felt like I was out of energy or needed to sleep. I just kept going like the energizer bunny. I was always pumped because I was doing what I loved.

Contrast that with something I dislike, project planning. I have a passionate dislike for Gantt charts, project management timelines, and SWOT analyses (Strengths, Weaknesses,

Opportunities, and Threats). I would find creative ways to avoid them at all costs. I miss deadlines. I find other projects to focus on. I get distracted with anything else just to avoid sitting down and putting all that stuff together.

If you judged me by how I do project planning, you would think I am the most disorganized person in the world.

On one side, I look like a tireless worker; on the other side, I'm a lazy and procrastinating employee. *Which one is right?*

I'd say both of them but they aren't a full representation of who I am and what I am worth.

Let's use a more common analogy. In the self-help, personal branding and success habits industry people love to quote the research that concluded people who exercise and are in great shape are more likely to succeed. Hence, companies and experts pushed the idea that looking athletic will lead to success.

Well, have they ever considered that the reason athletic people succeed has more to do with the mindset required to be fit than the fact they look strong?

Being physically fit requires discipline, hard work, strategy, skill, and confidence to overcome obstacles. These are all requirements to succeeding in life.

It's so easy to say I am...

- Clumsy
- Stupid
- Smart
- Strange
- Confident

- Insecure
- etc.

Feel free to make your list.

We love to categorize people based on their observed behaviors as if they are irrefutable proof of who they are. But *if behaviors were a direct definition of who we are, there couldn't be a chance for us to change how we do things or to learn new ways to express ourselves.*

If you made decisions about me based on how I operated eight years ago, you would make plenty of wrong predictions about my future and my personality.

My résumé no longer reflects who I am today. I have changed the way I think and behave in most of life's situations. I am not the person I was eight years ago. I am probably not the same person I was three years ago.

The phrase "**I AM**" implies permanence. Since we can choose and modify how to behave, **our behaviors are nothing more than a description of our choices at a specific moment.**

We are much more than our actions.

Which now brings me to the 4th and final thing we are not.

#4 - I Am Not My Thoughts

This one was the most challenging for me and probably the one my clients struggle with the most.

This is a struggle because we spend talking to ourselves 24x7. Our thoughts show up and there's nothing we can do about it. Hence, we have a choice to ignore, distract, or engage with them.

Since our consciousness allows us to think about us thinking about ourselves, and so on, it is easy to personify our thinking in such a way we believe we are the ones doing the thinking.

The philosopher René Descartes, is famously attributed the statement "*cogito ergo sum.*" **I think therefore I am.**

I can argue that René is right in how the universe works. The way I think has the power to shape my beliefs. What I believe affects how I feel about things. And, how I feel propels me to react or respond so it creates my results in this physical world. **I think, therefore I become.**

Thought > Emotion > Action > Results

To use my associate actuary example from before, the self-doubt was directly tied to the series of thoughts I was having about the physical experience. Here's the overview of the sequence of events:

1. I stop pursuing my fellowship certification level.
2. Several months later, my peers pass more exams and quickly get promoted.
3. We all have the same responsibilities.
4. I start thinking...
   a. Why am I not equally recognized and compensated when I do the same job?
   b. Is it all about having more exams?
   c. I should have done better
   d. What a dumb decision, why am I so lazy?
   e. Maybe, I'm not as smart as the rest
   f. I always start something and never finish it

Similar patterns of thought continued to repeat for at least eight months after I stopped taking exams.

I believed myself to be less valuable than others. Such is the power of thinking patterns and constant repetition.

Fortunately, I had resources and people in my life who helped me break the cycle.

Let's take a bird's eye view of this idea that we are not what we think.

- Who's doing the thinking?
- Where are thoughts coming from?
- Who is experiencing the thought?
- Who has the thought?
- Who gets to decide what to do with them?
- Who gives them power?

You guessed it! I am. I am the one who's experiencing these thoughts and creating the patterns of thinking.

In short, we are more than our thoughts. We are like a space through which ideas come by and we can choose to see them and let them go or act on them.

Juan, I See Your Point But...

You may be at a point where you are considering going through this process of challenging the labels, behaviors, appearance, and thinking but something may be getting in the way.

When I started the process, I was scared. I feared the emptiness. By the time I had my "living undercover" epiphany, I was convinced following other people's well-meaning advice would not guarantee my success, but I feared the unknown.

"If am not any of these things, what is left?" **was my thinking.** Nothing? Where do I even begin?

The first lesson I had to learn on my journey was to be at peace with not knowing what was coming next and not know how to describe myself. It was about humbling myself enough to accept starting a new life and entering the process of exploration, discovery, and creation.

It felt like I was entering limbo. Like being inside a pitch-black room with my eyes open and not seeing even one inch away from my eyes.

Have you ever been in that situation? How does it feel?

What helped me embrace the unknown was recognizing that by letting go of those attachments I was now free to choose whichever card I wanted to play and enter the learning process.

Entering a situation with the objective to discover rather than being right or succeed is an empowering feeling.

The beauty of having a baby as I write this book, is the ability to see in action what took a *"life crisis"* for me to discover.

There are moments in which my daughter stays alone in a dark room. Yes, she may cry a little, but you know what happens after a few minutes? She explores. She moves around, picks things up, touches other things, makes noises, tests, tries, and continues the process until someone shows up. She goes on a continuous study of the world. She discovers things she enjoys doing, things she prefers to ignore, and things she wants to play with.

In the midst of darkness, she finds a way to express herself despite the darkness and fear of being alone.

That's the power of a growth and discovery mindset. That's what this first step of passionately challenging everything I thought I knew about myself taught me.

Your Mission If You Choose to Accept It

Here's your invitation to take some practical steps to implement the previous concepts.

Find your style. If you want to start with an outline, here's what I did.

Step #1 - Make Your List of Things You Identify With

My preference is to use handwriting because there's a hand and mind connection that technology has not been able to replace. There's something about literally writing ideas down that channels a certain energy that the digital world cannot replace, yet.

What you will write down is everything that comes to mind when you fill-in-the-blanks the phrase: **I AM** _____

If that is too broad of a scope, you can narrow it down by framing your mind towards the categories we talked about: things, possessions, labels, titles, behaviors, personality, thoughts, activities, appearance, catch phrases, etc.

To be more specific, you can think of the different roles you play in life: profession, family, church, finances, friends, etc.

The choice is yours. I found the simplest thing for me to do, at first, was to just list many things in 10 minutes.

I AM...

- fat
- generous
- Impatient
- a good listener
- smart
- a servant
- etc.

There is no right answer to this process. This is an exercise of awareness.

You can choose to write for as long or short as you want. However, I encourage you to write for at least 10 minutes. Even if you run out of ideas, keep writing whatever comes to mind.

When the time runs out, clean up the list by removing the statements that make little sense and store them on a different list in case a new thought triggers later that may connect to those random phrases.

> Note: as you clean the list, this is not about judging whether a statement is right or wrong, you are just arranging things so the statements that apply to the I AM statement are taken to the next step.

Step #2 - What Are The Implications Of Each Item On The List?

Once you clean the list, the next stage is to reflect on the implications of each item. This is not a grading process but more of a discovery journey.

The intent of this step is to become aware of what does the item imply about the person who identifies with it. Pay attention to the 3rd person approach in the statement. Remove yourself from the exercise by thinking the items on the list are someone else's list.

Thus, take the time to pick one item at a time and answer the question: **what does this item say about the person that identifies with it?**

Again, there's no need to be perfect with your answers and you aren't supposed to be rating yourself. The objective is to help you learn of boundaries created by the I AM statements.

By now, you may have subconsciously created a picture of how you have defined yourself. But there's no need to pass judgment. You are an observer. You are learning of the full picture of the identity formed by the collection of your I AM statements.

Step #3 - Reject First

You will now go through each item on the list and ask yourself this: **if this [insert item] was no longer part of my life, how would I truly feel after setting it free?**

What you may notice when going through this exercise is that some items you will feel like a weight has been lifted off your shoulders. For others, you may feel like a part of you is going away and you'll fight to keep it.

But the surprising part of the exercise is that there will be many instances in which you will be neutral. You may think things like,

- But if I let that go xxx will happen
- People say I should...

- That would be nice to have
- People won't recognize me without this...
- I refuse to let this go...
- etc.

These are most likely inserted into your life out of fear, obligation, or a nice-to-have. While they may not be wrong, these are the items that should be challenged and proven valid before accepting them again into your life.

These neutral items are the ones I fight off daily because the ego is cunning, but no need to panic. This is a discovery journey not a grading system.

All you have to do in this step is identify how you would feel if the item is removed from your life:

1. Was it a weight lifted?
2. Something I absolutely don't want to let go? Or,
3. A mixed feeling?

Step #4 - Start The Discovery Process

The next logical step from here is to continue to the next phase of the framework: **Courageously Discover Your Light.**

At this point of the exercise, you have probably developed an idea of where to begin the validation process for which cards should make up your playing hand. While this exercise shines a light on which cards to pick back up, don't commit yourself to it, yet. Allow yourself the chance to continue exploring and validating everything you have written down.

Feel free to spend more time expanding on your notes. And when you are 80% or more ready to explore, continue on to the next chapter.

"You can only hide from yourself in the noise, but not in the quiet. If you truly want to get to know yourself, then get rid of the distractions.

If you want to really understand what has been holding you back, then simply and calmly focus your full attention within, and observe."

~Bryant McGill

Chapter 4: The Purpose Suit – Start With Why

Ever more people today have the means to live,
but no meaning to live for.

~Viktor Frankl

We ended our last discussion with an exercise to increase our level of awareness about the things we use to identify ourselves.

We had a list with what we use to identify ourselves and we asked the question, *"how would I truly feel if this item is no longer part of my life?"*

This question helped us segment the list into three buckets: a weight lifted, a must have, or a mixed feeling.

We also agreed to avoid committing to the results of this exercise regardless of how aligned it may be with our way of being.

Remember, there is no right or wrong answer, you are simply keeping the options open because the intent behind *Step #1 of the Greatness Within Framework* is to make room for what is a reflection of you.

Now, we begin the process of *"picking up the cards."*

Where to Begin: Google It!

It sounds like common sense but is not something one would automatically do.

The next step in this framework is to **courageously discover your light.** It's not necessarily about getting from the outside but exploring within us to identify which cards we should pick back up.

Your first reaction, like mine, could be to search on Google for something like "how to discover yourself." This would return about 1.4 Billion results in less than .6 seconds.

It only takes skimming through the results for a few minutes to realize that everyone has an opinion on what you should do to discover yourself but there are four areas mentioned frequently. To continue with the deck of cards analogy, *I'll refer to them as the four suits of courageously discovering your light.*

1. Have a purpose
2. Have a vision or a dream
3. Find what you are good at
4. Know what you value

Notice they are all internal questions. No one can decide for you what goes in your four suits. People will try to tell you what you "should do" but, remember, if you are reading this and you are still searching, it's because what people have told you so far hasn't worked.

Hence, this step of the framework focuses on helping you discover your answers.

In my experience, the top results of my Google search didn't help. My solution came from a personal development book called *"The 15 Invaluable Laws of Growth"* by John C. Maxwell.

This book changed my life not with its great content but because every chapter came with an introspection or application exercise at the end.

It was by reflecting and testing ideas that I found the answers to the four areas above.

What I share in these pages is strongly influenced by what I learned from going through John's book.

One More Thing: Your Internal Compass

Many ask me, *"how would I know which one is the right answer?"* when going through the exercises described in this book.

Before sharing my answer, I'd like to reiterate there is no right or wrong in this process. Hence, to avoid confusion, I propose that any insinuation of a *"right"* or *"wrong"* action be understood as **aligned** or **not aligned** to avoid falling into analysis paralysis.

While each person is different, I have found with my coaching clients that there's usually a sensation that identifies the proper path forward whether it makes sense or not.

As you go through this journey, you'll be tempted to overanalyze what you think and do. You'll try to gather more information. You'll seek advice from all types of experts in your life. You'll want to join personal development courses. You'll read more books. You'll build pros and cons lists. You'll want a robust statistical model to determine the right answer.

Here's my opinion on this approach: *relatively speaking, all that stuff is nice to have but not necessary.*

When I'm coaching someone, there are clear emotional and physical signs that the person has found the answer. *So, what's the answer?*

It has happened with me and all the clients I have had and it is better described by a sensation of expansion or contraction.

The aligned answers create a sense of expansion even in the presence of fear and doubt. It's a combination of fear and excitement at the same time. It is generally felt around the middle section of your body close to your heart.

The misaligned answers create a sense of contraction and rarely come with positive statements. It's a mixture of judgment, worry, fear, doubt, and stress. It is commonly felt above the shoulders around the neck area.

Now, is this a bulletproof scientific method for making life decisions? That's up for debate.

Everything can benefit from planning, analysis, and an execution process. The observation here is that life-changing decisions start with a feeling of expansion...

- ...a weight lifted off my shoulders
- ...a warm feeling in my chest
- ...an instant sense of peace and clarity
- ...a level of excitement that overcomes all doubts
- ...an inexplicable sense of security even when there's no clue what's next

As you go through this journey, I encourage you to pay attention to your internal compass. The part of you that seems to know all the right answers but that rarely screams or overpowers. The more you pay attention to it, the more you'll be able to test it and hone your intuitive decision-making process.

The Purpose Suit: Start With Why

Simon Sinek, in his book, *"Start With Why"*, makes the case that human fulfillment revolves around knowing and expressing the reason for our existence. He makes the argument that humans are driven by "Why" and companies who learn to express their "Why" clearly, attract their ideal customers and achieve great success.

Simon's message is one that connected with me a lot because I found myself always trying to figure out the purpose behind everything. I not only want to be purposeful in what I do, but I also spend a lot of energy trying to understand why other people do what they do.

It's my experience that life goes a lot better when we have a driving reason behind it all. The key is becoming aware of that reason.

To quote my mentor Paul Martinelli, "purpose is the reason why you do what you do and it's what you allow to be the filter through which you make all decisions."

Whether you know it or not, there's a driven force behind everything you do and all that you are. Hence, identifying your purpose statement is probably a good place to start for defining yourself, stop seeking validation, and thrive your way.

Four ideas to consider about finding your purpose

1. **It's not an exam.** While you may be tempted to approach this exercise like a do or die college exam, permit yourself to say "I don't know." There's is no urgency to finish on time or get the right answer. Chances are you'll need months and years to refine your purpose statement. Know that it is okay to start with an outline.

2. **It's a process, not an event.** My current purpose statement took 10 years to develop. That doesn't mean it will take you that long to figure it out. It means you should treat this as a journey not a once and done deal.

3. **Action refines the answer.** Once you have a starting point, the more you explore it and intentionally align with it, the more you'll be able to clarify what motivates you to operate in this world. The key is to keep moving.

4. **A trusted partner.** All journeys are better with company. Find someone to share your findings and continue learning. Pick someone who will take the role of helping you explore and encourage progress rather than a passive listener.

What's So Important About Purpose?

Having a purpose helps set boundaries for your life. It doesn't have to be clear initially, it just has to be a path to follow. You may start with a broad statement, but as you go through life seeking to identify your driving force, your purpose statement will get specific.

To use myself as an example, here's the evolution of my purpose statement:

1. **I want to be different.** I grew up with my dad always asking *"Do you want to be like everyone else?"* Hence, I started intending to be different. It's what led me to become an actuary. Why? Because it was a career I never heard of and it wasn't offered in Panama. It was different.

2. **I want to be different by helping others.** This came from my curiosity to find ways I could help people in ways I thought were different from what others did.

3. **I want to be different in my way** *(I challenge the status quo)*. Over time, I focused on using my specific talents to stand out from the crowd and serve others.

4. **I want to help others be different** *(I help others challenge the status quo)*. In this stage, my focus shifted to helping others be different by using their talents and interests.

5. **I use powerful questions to help you break through self-limiting beliefs and move closer to your full potential.** This statement came up by combining the experiences and findings from #3 and #4. I knew my talents and passions. I knew significantly more about myself than 10 years prior. Most of the progress came from intentionally seeking to refine why I did what I did.

6. **I help you discover your capacity to create a life worthy of you.** This is my statement and a summary of the prior phrases. This statement fuels what I do. I notice how it shows in my daily interactions with people. I have this inherent drive to work with people who want to evolve and express themselves fully. And, I do all I can to facilitate their progress.

If there's one thing to note from the evolution of my purpose statement is that I didn't venture to give myself a purpose. I went out to become aware of it.

Regardless of the approach you take to find your purpose, know it doesn't change, we simply increase our awareness of it.

I share this to reinforce the need to approach this as a discovery journey rather than a goal to meet or a prize to be won. As you move with intention, the *"creation"* will take care of itself.

> *As you move with intention, the creation*
> *will take care of itself.*

How To Find Your Purpose

Rather than telling you the exact process I used, I share three exercises I went through so you can personalize your experience.

My suggested approach:

1. Pick one
2. Give it a few tries
3. Observe the outcomes
4. Keep what resonates most
5. Rinse and repeat until you have a statement

What worked for me was a combination of these three exercises. While I do believe they work, you may discover your unique exercise as you walk your path.

Option #1 - The Practical Baby Steps

This method is better suited for individuals who are stumped with increasing self-awareness and confidently claim they have no idea of what they like or where to begin.

No need to be self-conscious, this is a valid circumstance so don't feel like something is wrong.

A high-level description of the process goes something like this:

1. Start by pursuing something you are most interested in.
2. This will lead you to identify and develop skills and talents.
3. As you use your talents to add value to others, you'll develop a passion for specific activities.
4. Finally, as you reflect on the experiences you are passionate about, you'll discover a common driving force behind it.
5. The reason for pursuing these experiences with a passion is your purpose statement.

The practical description of the process could be:

1. Brainstorm a list of any activities that create a sense of interest for you to learn about or do. Three things to note about the list:
   a. It doesn't matter how silly it may sound, just make a list.
   b. The list can include past activities or things you have heard about but never done.
   c. The objective is to give yourself options.
2. Once the list is done, you pick the item that generates the most interest and engage with it.
3. Set some goals related to the activity focused on improving your skill and applying it in your life.
4. As you gain experience with it, inherently notice whether this activity is something you can use extensively in your life or simply a nice experience to share stories about.

5. If you determine you have a talent for the activity, you'll develop a passion for utilizing it to help yourself and others.
6. As time goes by, your passion will lead you to other skills and experiences.
7. The accumulation of experiences will highlight a common thread of areas in which you can add value to others and lead you to identify a summary statement for why you do what you do.
8. The latter is your working purpose statement.
9. If at any point in your journey you determine the activity is not your thing, then you go back to the original list and start with something else.

In summary: *Pursue an area of interest > Identify & develop talents and skills > Leads into discovering passions > The combination highlights your purpose*

This process works because it focuses on acting without losing momentum with analysis paralysis. All it takes is evaluation as you gain new experiences, to identify what is an interest that can be pursued forever versus a shiny object that gained temporary attention.

Option #2 - The Infinite Why Loop

This one reminds me of children who like to ask an infinite number of questions about a subject just to learn about it. You can probably guess how it works.

I heard this method numerous times but never paid attention to it because it seemed dumb. It wasn't until I educated myself on coaching techniques that I understood the power of staying curious.

While many people get defensive when asked *"Why"* there are different ways of arriving at the same question.

There's something powerful about staying with a problem for longer periods and exploring what's behind it all. To use the cliché phrase, *"it's like peeling the layers of an onion."*

The process:
1. Identify an activity you enjoy doing or something that seems to always give you energy.
2. Once identified, start asking yourself *"Why do you enjoy it so much?"*
3. Regardless of the answer, continue asking *"And why is that?"* in relation to the given answer.
4. Do this about 5-7 times or until you come up with an answer that creates a visceral response. A response that may provoke you to act right away.
5. Whichever statement produced the response, is a good starting point for your purpose statement.

It is a straightforward process but if you engage with it and permit yourself to explore, you'll come up with a very good starting point.

Here's an example using my experience:
1. Why did you become an actuary? Because I wanted to be different.
2. Why? Because I wanted to stand out and being an actuary is very different because it's not even an available degree in Panama.
3. And, why is it important for you to stand out? Because I like being an individual; a person that creates their destiny and leaves a mark.

4. Why? Because there's something powerful about creating your path.
5. And why is that? Maybe, because I have this belief that everyone came here for a reason and deserves to create the life they are meant to live.

While this is not the exact process I followed, I have used it several times with positive results.

Bonus: The process can be more effective if you find yourself a partner with whom you can be transparent and not feel judged. The role of your partner is to continue asking "why" questions until you arrive at your powerful answer.

Option #3 - A Trip Down Memory Lane

This method is probably the one that takes the most effort since it requires reflecting on your life as far back as you can. But it is also a useful way to identify the theme of your life and how your purpose shows up.

I heard of this exercise from Simon Sinek in his book *Finding Your Why*. What follows is paraphrased from the book.

The process:
1. Select your preferred writing canvas (i.e., Paper, whiteboard, floor, wall, chalkboard, etc.)
2. Start by drawing a timeline. Choose your version of it. The simplest option is to draw a horizontal line representing your life's timeline as of today.
3. In the top half, you write or plot your strongest and emotionally charged positive memories and/or experiences you have had so far.

4. Conversely, you'll plot your strongest and emotionally charged negative memories and/or experiences on the bottom half.

5. You can represent the intensity of the memory by their distance from the horizontal line. No need to be precise. It's all subjective.

6. Once you have plotted your memories, you start with the most intense memories and identify what made them significant.

7. Do this review for both the positive and negative memories. Focus on the most intense memories first.

8. Once you have assessed the most intense memories, review your descriptions and answer this question: *what connects them all?*

9. Once you have come up with an answer or series of answers, test the responses with the other memories you plotted.

10. The answer that aligns best or generates the greatest instinctual connection is the start of your purpose statement.

For this process, it is also helpful to have a partner that can help you explore your memories and help you identify the common thread.

One of the practical uses of this exercise is the visualization of key memories/experiences of your life. The resulting chart helps frame the mind to look for connections and go back in time.

What To Do After You Have A Purpose Statement

You now have three tools to identify your purpose statement.

Many people write their purpose statement, file it, and forget about it. Similar to how companies have off-site meetings to come up with mission and vision statements and pretend the piece of paper will make it all a reality.

Be an action taker.

The next step is to use your statement as a foundation for how you approach life going forward.

It's a simple process that requires regular times for reflection about what you do and why you do everything in your life.

Recall my mentor Paul's definition of purpose, "it is the reason why you do what you do and it's what you allow to be the filter through which you make all decisions."

The reflection exercise is straight forward:

1. List all the things you are committed to
2. For each item on the list, read your purpose statement, and ask, *"how does this "item" relate to my purpose statement?"*
3. Go through the entire list before moving to the next step.
4. With your entire list assessed, review the answers, and see if there's a pattern.
   a. Either the activities aren't related or your purpose statement can be refined.
   b. Most likely, there will be activities you aren't sure why you are doing them. Those are contenders for limitation, delegation, or elimination.
5. With the review done, you can now move into the proactive stage and ask *"what are new activities I can do to express my purpose more fully?"*

6. Go through this reflection exercise at least once a month, initially.

Remember, this is not about being right. It's about exploring and refining. As you practice this application exercise, you'll increase your awareness and notice why some things excite you and others feel like a pain in the butt.

The key is to be intentional and not archive your discoveries hoping everything will change as you go.

Here's a bonus outcome of moving purposefully, you'll start identifying with who you should spend time and who you should invest time with. There's something about moving with a purpose that starts attracting and repelling the right people.

In the next chapter, we explore ways to identify the ideal version of your life as we discuss the second suit: **vision**.

Chapter 5: The Vision Suit - The Highest Expression of You

Our only limitation, within reason, is the development and use of our imagination.

~Napoleon Hill

The buzzword here is **vision.** It's the ultimate goal. When the individual can experience the byproduct of their essence showing up in the world.

For many, myself included, having a vision is a concept preached by the gurus of the world that can be challenging to implement.

Here are a few of my beliefs and thoughts about vision.

I believe most people struggle with having a vision for their lives because it has been schooled out of them.

Have you ever met a kid without imagination? Have you ever engaged in conversation with a kid about "what they want to do when they grow up?"

I think we all have done it but we rarely pay attention to what happens in that conversation.

Children are masters at vision setting. Most are very detailed when describing what they would do and why they want to do it. **They never stop to consider how difficult or unrealistic their dream may be.**

But who decides this dream is unrealistic? Who determines what the child is saying is a thing for movies and fantasy books?

As children grow and get indoctrinated by the school systems and the limiting beliefs of their parents doing their best to raise responsible adults, those dreams slowly fade away and are classified as daydreaming or child's play.

- You are too old for that kind of thing
- That's not the way the world works
- That's not what grown-ups do.
- And how are you going to do that?
- But that makes no money
- etc.

Sounds familiar?

Combine these phrases told by influential adults in our lives with the school system pushing us to pick the safe careers, to not fail the tests and to always have a plan following proven steps, and we have an excellent recipe to numb our most powerful tool to create a life worthy of us. **With our imagination gone, can life truly be fun and exciting?**

Take a moment to review all the things that exist that weren't possible a handful of years ago.

- There are 11-year-old kids making thousands of dollars playing video games
- Millionaire toddlers that review toys on live video.

- We can video chat with anyone in the world in a matter of seconds regardless of our location
- Cars that drive themselves
- Drones delivering packages
- Working from home for overseas companies without losing connectivity
- Making money from social media activity
- We can print 3-dimensional objects like hammers, ventilators, houses, etc.

These things weren't even possible 10 years ago. And some were considered impossible. And yet, here we are.

Someone dared enough to visualize all these things happening and they did.

To quote my distant mentor Simon Sinek, *"vision is the ability to talk about the future with such clarity it is as if we are talking about the past."*

How Do I Filter The Noise Around Vision Setting?

With the importance of vision, I think we sometimes take it too seriously and set ourselves up for failure.

As adults, we would take the advice of the experts on the field and assume we are supposed to have a crystal-clear vision before we take the very first step.

It is here where an important distinction needs to be made. There needs to be clarity but not necessarily a robust and thorough plan around it.

I can have a vision but sometimes it is not a detailed vision, just a clear one. It is a definite goal.

Not everyone gets those movie-like visions of an ideal future right away. I see this with coaching clients where it can take several sessions to extract what they want out of life.

Allow me to illustrate what I mean with a personal anecdote.

In February 2017, I played with the idea of hosting a leadership development event for anyone interested. It was something I wanted to do for several years but never considered because the company I worked for already had a curriculum available to those in management positions.

What was interesting about the situation is that the company offered many events annually for different subjects but never for leadership concepts. If there were any events, they were reserved for the V.I.P.

I wanted to host one open to anyone interested regardless of their title. The reason I wanted to host the event is that I saw a gap in the development of the employees interested in leadership or aspired to manage a team. And, I wanted the opportunity to help others define their leadership style and path.

Recall my purpose statement, "I help you discover your capacity to create a life worthy of you."

In April 2017, I took a leap of faith and did it. I didn't know how to do it, I didn't have a meeting room, I didn't have a budget, I didn't know the theme, and I didn't know who would be the speakers.

What I had was a definite idea of hosting a leadership conference for anyone who wanted to attend regardless of their title or seniority.

As the weeks go by, I thought about what I wanted it to look like, what I wanted participants to take away from it, who I wanted to show up, what topics should be covered, and visualizing how many attendees I wanted.

Over time, the vision got clearer and clearer.

As I shared the vision for the event, help showed up. I found volunteer speakers. Someone helped me booking the rooms. Others helped spread the word. Another team offered to help record the sessions.

In less than four months, everything worked out.

Allowing myself to dream about the opportunity and visualize what I wanted out of it made it possible for 300 people to receive the training they would have never gotten through the company.

Most importantly, I proved to myself that dreams do come true when we give them the time and energy to flourish.

There are a few things to highlight in my story.

1. **Intentional thinking time is required:** Emerson is paraphrased as saying, *"where your focus goes, energy flows."* The more time one gives to think about what they want, the clearer the vision.
2. **Definite decision:** I had to commit to the decision to go for the leadership conference before my brain worked towards it. Often, I have tried to "keep my options open" which ended up with nothing getting done.
3. **Specificity over time:** It took several months of thinking about it for my vision to get clear. It started with a definite goal that ended with a clear picture of the event.

How does this apply to you?

As you start the journey, you might be tempted to consume more information and prepare for what's coming. You may focus on getting it right and listening to other people's advice. But all you'll be doing is adding noise to the process when all that is required is focused time, a decision, and taking the first step.

You filter through the noise by giving time to the wisdom within you to speak and refine your steps as you move towards that definite goal.

When you know what you want and see it,
you'll be willing to pay the price and
overcome challenges to achieve it.

~Jon Gordon

The One Thing to Overcome Before Setting Your Vision

The Internet has no absence of resources about vision setting. From worksheets to extensive video seminars, it is possible to find something that will fit any personality in the world. Yet, *why is it that most people struggle to do it?*

The more clients I coach the clearer the obstacle that gets in the way.

Johnny sits in front of me and shares his situation. He tells me about his circumstances and the things he would like to change. He talks about wanting something better. But he seems vague when describing what he wants.

I take a moment to process what has been said and respond with a simple question, "Johnny, suppose you are a few years into the future and all these gaps you talk about have been resolved. What does that life look like?"

With clarity and confidence, Johnny says "I don't know."

I have not kept count of how often I have heard or used that response. *"I don't know."*

Take a few seconds to reread the scenario above and pretend you are Johnny. *What's your answer to my question?*

What I have found is that few people have a descriptive answer to the question right away. Why? Because we seem to suffer from the historian or reporter syndrome.

What I have noticed is that the answer is not really *"I don't know."* What we mean to say is *"I don't know HOW!"*

A response that's natural.

In Johnny's situation, when asked about what he wants for his life, the mind automatically enters the historian or reporter mode. It functions something like this:

1. Received question or problem to solve: "What do you truly want Johnny?"
2. In milliseconds, the mind identifies "what" Johnny wants and figures out how to get it.
3. It looks at past experiences (Johnny's history)
4. It looks at his skills, money, and resources. (Johnny's current news)
5. It determines nothing like that exists in Johnny's world.
6. Hence, it doesn't know how to do it.
7. Finally, the signal is sent to respond "I don't know"

It's a perfectly logical process to determine the answer except for the mistake of trying to use the past and present to determine the future. It's a process that guarantees the answer to always be "I don't know."

Setting up a vision is about creating something that hasn't been done before in our lives. If we haven't done it before, there's no way for us to know exactly how to do it going forward. If we knew how to do it, we would already have it.

The solution: *suspend the requirement of knowing how to do it.*

A few years ago, I read a few articles about how GPS technology works. Specifically, how to determine the best driving route.

Route mapping software requires us to tell the device where we want to go and where we are.

Most people don't know how the route is determined. When the programmers were testing the algorithms, they noticed that if you figured out the route from A to B, the program will easily get lost and never reach the destination. But when they reversed engineer the route, the program always got from A to B.

Interestingly, this reverse engineering approach is also how the mind works for figuring out our ideal version of the future.

The original approach of determining the driving route from A to B is similar to one trying to figure out how to get somewhere we have never been before. Similarly, the reverse engineering method of determining the route from B to A is how vision setting works best.

We must first visualize the ideal version of our future and then walk backwards to figure out how to get there. *First, we set a clear vision. Second, we figure out how.*

The vision must be independent of how.

Recall my anecdote about hosting the leadership conference. I decided I wanted to do it, gave attention to describing what I wanted to happen, shared the vision with others, and the "HOW" figured itself out.

Suspend the requirement of knowing how.

~Paul Martinelli

The Advantage of Being A Child

Something is fascinating about children who haven't been programmed to worry about getting things right and plan everything.

One day, I'm doing some customer support when I hear the sound of a light switch flipping on and off. I kept minding my business until I heard something tumbling down, a huge thump, and then wailing.

The baby had fallen.

It turns out, she had climbed up the stroller parked in the hallway by the light switch. She was standing on the stroller turning the light on and off.

The stroller didn't have the brakes on and, as she leaned against the wall, the stroller moved away from the wall. Thus, making room for her to fall.

I would have never guessed she could climb the stroller.

Fortunately, she was okay.

Setting the new parent stupid mistake aside, consider what my daughter went through.

As a responsible parent, you could think of all the reasons she should have never tried to climb the stroller.

- The stroller seat is about two feet off the ground.
- She can't reach the seat edge.
- She doesn't know how to climb stairs.
- The light switch is about four feet off the floor
- She is, roughly, 19 inches tall.

Somehow, she saw the light switch and thought to herself, *"I should go find out what that does!"* Without hesitation, she sees the stroller and climbs it so she can reach the light switch. It couldn't have been over two minutes.

She did all of that never considering she could fall, she didn't know how to climb, or that it could be dangerous. She simply went for it with a simple purpose: **the desire to play and discover.**

The latter is the second requirement for working on your vision statement. *Once you have suspended the requirement of knowing how to make your vision a reality, you must give yourself permission to play and discover.*

As you attempt the following vision setting exercises, I'm encouraging you to suspend the requirement of knowing how to do it and permit yourself to have fun.

Let's begin.

Three Ways to Formulate The Ideal Expression Of Your Purpose (a.k.a. Vision)

There are plenty of vision setting resources on the Internet. The ones I share here are the ones I have used myself and with my coaching clients.

Similar to the purpose statement exercises, give each one a try and then pick the one that aligns with your style the most.

Remember, give yourself permission to have fun and suspend the need to know how to do whatever comes to mind as you go through the exercises.

Option #1 - Authentic Journaling

Relax, this is not one of those "dear diary" practices. While it does involve writing, the focus of this approach is to let your unconscious mind reveal to you what you want. It's a way to let your imagination come out and play.

I implemented this exercise when trying to decide where to focus my time in expressing my purpose. Now, I share it with you.

Rules of this exercise

- **Write as fast as you can.** This is done to prevent your critical thinking from stumping your creativity and imagination.
- **Forget about spelling and grammar.** No one else is going to read these pages. Write with enough clarity so you can review what you say later. You don't have to get it right.
- **Write down everything that comes to mind even if it's unrelated to the question you'll answer.** This helps maintain the flow of creativity and build momentum.

Keep writing because the editing can be done much later during your review time.

- **Use the present or past tense.** Even though you'll be writing about your future, using the present or past tense helps with suspending the requirement of knowing how to do it. To the brain, something in the present or past is already in existence so there's no need to figure out how to do it.

- **Voice is acceptable but pen and paper seem to work best.** Some people are better communicators when they speak. Plus, one can speak faster than writing. It's okay to voice record your answers to this exercise but it's strongly encouraged to try this in writing first. There's a mind-body connection that becomes present during the writing process that cannot be replicated with voice. But the objective is to extract the ideas from your mind so do what works best for you.

The journaling process:

1. Set aside time to focus on this task. You can start with five minutes a day. If you can go longer, then do so.
2. Make sure there aren't any distractions.
3. Find a pen and a notepad.
4. Before you write, take 2-3 slow deep breaths and allow your body to slow down and relax.
5. Now, take 30-60 seconds to quickly jot down anything you think needs to get done before the day is over. This list is to let your brain know you will not forget so that you can give full attention to this journaling task.
6. In a new piece of paper, at the top of the page, write down the question you will be focusing on for the day. You can

choose whichever question you'd like to answer as it relates to creating the ideal version for your life. Some sample questions are:

    a. What kind of life do I truly want?

    b. It's three years in the future, what does my life look like?

    c. What would I love to be doing with my life?

7. As you write the question at the top of the page, start the clock and write down whatever comes to mind to answer that question. It doesn't matter what comes up, write it down as quickly as you can.

8. Repeat this process as many days as you like.

9. After a few rounds of this exercise, review what you have written and look for patterns. The pattern is the starting outline for your vision.

Why does it work?

The objective of this exercise is to temporarily pause the logical mind.

That's the importance of giving ourselves permission to play and write anything that comes to mind during the allotted time. In writing as fast as possible, the logical mind doesn't have time to catch up, which then lets our imagination get to work.

The less you think through the process, the easier it is to let your inner wisdom speak and share your true desires for your life.

Initially, it's normal to think what you write down is ridiculous and silly. Some things you come up with will sound so far off your reach that you'll be tempted to dismiss the entire exercise. It is in those moments where you have to remind yourself of these practices: suspend the requirement of knowing how to do it and permit yourself to play. You don't have to get it right.

Option #2: - The Wall of Dreams

I once listened to a summary of how Michael Phelps was trained by his coaches and mentors. In the audio, his coach talks about how he gave Michael a simple exercise. He said, *"before you go to bed, I want you to play the videotape."*

The line was a trigger for Michael to visualize his perfect race in vivid detail. Every night and before each race, he will *"play the videotape."* Judging by Michael's Olympic gold medals record, this technique worked well.

There's power in having a vehicle through which you visualize your life in perfect harmony. If writing is not your thing, maybe this method will help you unlock your creativity.

Let's remember the key practices: you don't need to know how to do it and you must permit yourself to play.

This exercise works because it removes you from the picture and it places you as the observer of a wonderful movie that just mirrors your life.

Let's give it a go.

The process in story form

>*Suppose you are inside a simple room. There's nothing inside of it, just you. You look around and the walls are painted in your favorite color. It gives you a sense of joy, excitement, and relaxation. It just puts you in a good mood.*

You are standing in front of the left side wall of the room. This wall represents your life until this point. There's no need to focus on it. You simply know everything you have experienced so far is represented on that wall.

Now, you look at the directly opposite wall. At this moment, you are a little too far to notice what's on it. You are curious. Hence, you walk towards the right-side wall. The closer you get to the wall the clearer the images and the more vivid they appear.

Now, you want to know what's on the wall. As you get close enough to see everything clearly, you notice you are watching someone's life.

It turns out, this wall represents your ideal future. In the middle of the wall, is the main event. It's your fully aligned life playing in front of you. Surrounding this main image are the highlights of your life regarding the areas of your life you value most. Whatever you can think of, it's there.

Pay attention to the wall. Focus on the events playing on it. See and feel yourself there.

Now, as you look near the wall, a chair and desk appear.

On the desk, there's a notepad and your favorite writing instrument, a voice recorder, and a video camera.

Pick your preferred method and document everything you see on that right side wall. Don't worry. You can reference the wall anytime you want. Just focus on documenting what you see so you can take it with you everywhere you go.

You can write it down. You can record your voice describing what you see. You can record a video of yourself describing the wall.

You can't go wrong with any method. You only have to document what you see.

Remember, there's no need to know how you got there. You simply focus on documenting what you see.

Once you are finished, you now have a starting point for your full expression of your purpose. You have a vision statement to help you focus your life as you move forward.

The final step in this exercise is to simply *"play the videotape."*

Continue referring to your recordings until the vision is so clear that there's no doubt of where you are headed.

No need to be perfect

If the first time you attempt this exercise the movie is fuzzy, don't fret. This is all about practice and having fun.

The entire objective of this exercise is to reconnect with your imagination and let your inner wisdom say what it needs to say. The more you practice the easier it is to visualize.

Option #3 - The Blissful Average Day

In contrast to the wall experience, this version places you at the center of the exercise. It's a concept that helps you remember your future. It's a way to tell yourself about the things that have happened or are happening in your ideal life.

Recall the key practices: you don't need to know how to do it and you are permitting yourself to play.

I have had experiences where the person gets hindered by creating a vision of an ideal state because they link "ideal" with "perfect." Since we have been trained to think perfect doesn't exist, the unconscious reaction is to think *"why even try this when I know perfect is not real?"*

Then, I read from Steve Chandler, one of the top coaches in the world, telling people to enjoy having an average day.

The reason behind it is that an average day doesn't come with the pressures of making everything efficient and effective. Since there's no need to be at their best, the individual stays relaxed and becomes more creative. This creates all the opportunities to stay productive and effect change.

Hence, the concept of the *blissful average day* to generate a vision statement.

The process:
Take a handful of deep and slow breaths to allow the mind to slow down and to release some stress.

Recall a moment in which you were the most joyful. A moment where everything seemed to go smoothly and everything came easy to you. Remember the feeling and stay with it.

> *With that high energy, suppose you have traveled in time to a future in which everything seems to go well for you. It doesn't matter how that happened; you are there.*

> *You just woke up. The day is just getting started and you get to do the same things you have been doing for some time now.*

> *Every day is your favorite day because you get to do what you love, you invest time with people who bring the best out of you, and you just move through your average day with bliss.*

Now, someone in your life has noticed the way things have been going for you and they want to know "What does your regular day look like?"

Thus, you document the "A day in the life of [insert your name]"

You grab your phone and record what's happening that day.

- *Who are you meeting*

- *The tasks you are up to*

- *What you do around the house*

- *What you do for work*

- *The things you love doing*

- *The meetings you have that day*

- *And, anything else that happens on your average day.*

You are as descriptive as possible because this person is truly intrigued by what you are doing.

No one has ever asked you to do this, so it's okay to be all over the place and ramble in the beginning. It will get better as you go throughout the day. Remember, they just want to see what you are doing. Whatever you are doing is fine.

It's your average day. No stress. No crazy demands. Just going through the normal routines and getting things done in total flow.

Now, we are back to the present moment. You have recorded your blissful average day. It shall serve you as a reminder of what you have accomplished. A reminder of something you can completely do.

Why this works

This method works because as you state your blissful average day in the present tense, the brain cannot distinguish between present or future. Whatever directives it gets, it will seek to accomplish.

This documentation serves as your north star for your journey going forward.

You now have three ways to describe your ideal expression of your purpose: authentic journaling, the wall of dreams, and the blissful average day.

The suggested next step would be to take some time to try the exercises and create your vision's first draft before moving on to the next chapter discussing **the tools that make you unique.**

Chapter 6: The Strengths Suit - The Toolkit That Makes You Unique

Society spends a lot of time, energy, and effort trying to convince us that to stand out we must mimic what other successful people are doing. This strategy is present everywhere and it feeds on the inherent need of humans to belong and to be special.

We grow in an environment that programs us to compare ourselves to everyone else. To measure success and happiness by the clothes we wear, the things we own, the titles we earn, and the accolades accumulated along the way.

It's a system that makes us believe our value comes from the outside and it leaves us constantly seeking approval and validation from the people we care about, our friends, our jobs, and our communities.

The Internet hasn't made it any easier to find ourselves. It has exacerbated the problem. We seek to stand out by copying what the influencers and gurus are doing.

In the process of all this mimicking, all we have done is create a fake persona that is a cookie-cutter replica of everyone else.

It's ironic. In our quest to be unique, we become a collage of other people's features.

The more you seek to be unique by copying other people's behaviors, models, and businesses, the more you are saying "NO" to yourself and seeking for validation that you are doing the right thing.

The worst of it all is that when you do get the validation, you may smile on the outside but feel empty inside.

It was a shallow win that came from modeling other people who are probably copying other people, too.

The more you own your voice and say yes to your behavioral quirks, your distinct thought patterns, and those activities that come so easy to you, the faster you add significant value to others.

That's when people start coming to you for help and pay you for what you do best.

The path to being unique and thriving your way is never to be found outside of you. It can only come from the greatness already within you.

Don Clifton, cofounder of the Gallup Organization, is often quoted as saying *"There is something you do better than 10,000 other people, and we just need to find what it is."*

Thus, this chapter is about giving you a way to identify what you can do better than 10,000 other people.

But before going there, it's important to distinguish between strengths and talents.

Talent Is Never Enough

"Talent is cheaper than table salt. What separates the talented individual from the successful one is a lot of hard work."

~Stephen King

It is common practice for people to interchange the words strength and talent. The problem is they are related but not the same.

The key distinction between the two is the intentional application and development of a skill.

Talent is just like knowledge. It has the potential to do great things but if you don't know how and when to apply it, it's worthless.

How many people do you know that are naturally talented at something but they don't seem to use it to make an impact with it?

A life worthy of us cannot be created without identifying, developing, and applying our talents to make a difference in the world.

I share three things I think hinder transforming our talents into a powerful skill.

Hindrance #1 - Society wants average
As far back as I can remember, I have been prompted to work on my weaknesses.

As a child, I was frequently asked about the low grades and the subjects I struggled with. As an adult, performance reviews and feedback were mostly focused on what I did wrong, what needed to improve, and what needed to stop.

I can only guess this societal practice is related to the natural fear that weakness used to mean death in the early days of human existence.

There's an inherent fear that if I am lacking in certain areas, I will appear weak to the "community" and therefore be removed from it. It's a survival mechanism that seems to push us to want to be liked by the group or risk "death" by being expelled from the tribe.

This thinking has affected me most of my life. I am constantly told I need to work on my delivery of communications; which is usually the politically correct way to tell me I am being rude, offensive, or that I sound like a know-it-all.

For years, I worked on cleaning up my delivery but the "wrong approach" feedback kept coming. Sooner or later, someone would repeat the same feedback giving no useful information. But I kept thinking it was my fault and I needed to change my style. I believed *"there was something wrong with me."*

I spent so much time trying to "fix" my delivery I neglected the areas in which I was very good. Which ended with me giving lackluster performance and a blend of mediocre skills.

It wasn't until a few years ago that I chose to focus on honing my talents and working around my weak spots that I saw positive results in my life and the lives of those I engaged with.

What I learned from those decades is simple: *it takes a lot of energy and effort to improve an area in which we lack talent but it's easy to significantly raise the skill level of an area we are naturally gifted to do.*

In my quest to fix my delivery, I neglected working on my talents. Thus, my speaking style may have gone from a three to a five but my strengths went from an eight to a six. The result was a forgettable performance.

I submit to you an alternative to working on your weaknesses: focus on your strengths and work around your gaps or partner with someone who can complement you.

> *I can do what you can't do, and you can do what I can't do; together we can do great things.*
>
> ~*Mother Teresa*

If you read the strategies from the most successful people in the world, you'll notice they all invested their time in the activities they do amazingly well and delegated the rest. This approach is preached by all the time management experts and strategists so I don't have to repeat those teachings because you have read and heard about them enough.

What I'm encouraging you to do is to set aside the pride and humble yourself enough to be okay with not being great at everything. Society will work hard to make you think that if you aren't great at everything, you'll fail.

Do not succumb to the temptation of becoming a "well-rounded" talent. The guaranteed way to thrive your way is to become so great at what you are naturally talented to do that no one else can do it as well as you do.

Hindrance #2 - Wanting to help everyone

This is my Achilles' heel. As a servant-minded individual, I dislike leaving people behind. I root for the underdog. I want everyone to succeed. Therefore, I think that everyone around me should be able to benefit from what I do.

Hence, I have tried learning many skills just because someone in my circle needed help with it. I did so even if the activity took me a lot of effort to learn and implement.

In my focus to help everyone, I became a jack of all trades and master of none. I was doing many things at a decent level but I wasn't known for a particular thing.

As you go through discovering your strengths, you must pay attention to where you are focusing your energy so you don't jump from learning one skill to another before you have mastered it. You'll have to resist the temptation to want to say yes to things that aren't aligned with your talents simply because you want to save face and appear helpful.

Yes, you may disappoint a few people along the way but, eventually, mastering your natural talents will create a greater impact because you will be working in areas where you are 10 instead of being good enough using your 6s-7s.

> *"Everybody is a genius. But if you judge a fish by its ability to climb a tree, it will live its whole life believing it is stupid."*
>
> *~Anonymous*

Hindrance #3 - Thinking strengths are microwavable.

Talent is a lot like knowledge. It has little value unless it is applied where it produces the greatest impact. Identifying how to apply knowledge takes time and experience. The same applies when transforming your talents into strengths.

Many talented individuals never amount to much in the world because they rarely take the time to explore, discover, and perfect their abilities.

The exercises shared later will help identify the areas in which you are talented but turning them into strengths will depend on how much effort you put into the process.

In my experience, developing strengths covers these four areas:

1. **Identifying the talents:** everyone is born with a natural ability for certain activities and ways of thinking but very few take the time to recognize them.
2. **Intentional application:** once a possible area of strength is identified, it must be applied and tested to validate it.
3. **Specificity:** strengths can be transferable but maximizing their impact depends on applying them in specific areas and roles.
4. **Regular audits:** a feedback loop is required for continuous improvement.

As you can see, this iterative process requires time and practice. It's unrealistic to think talent will become a strength the very first time it is used.

Once again, this is about the journey, not an immediate outcome.

Give yourself permission to explore and discover. There's no need to get it right and there's no way to get it wrong.

Becoming Aware of The Toolkit

Before going into the exercises, I thought it would be useful to share a practical example of how the strengths show up in daily life.

The first time I heard about the concept of "Strengths" was when I started my health insurance job. It was back when Gallup's StrengthsFinder tests and the employee engagement movement were gaining momentum.

The company had decided every new employee needed to take the assessment as part of their on-boarding process. The objective was to help each person succeed by allocating work based on their strengths.

I was so excited about the initiative and the possibility of having a tailored workload based on my strengths.

A few months into the job, I was disappointed. The initiative never happened. Like many things, the pressure of getting things done was more important than figuring out how to maximize each person's strengths.

Thus, I let it go and focused on just doing the work.

It wasn't until eight years later when I started charting my course that I finally paid attention to the idea of applying my strengths.

The more I delved into personal development, the more I noticed how I was unaware of how often I approach problems with the same set of skills.

My strengths were like my toolkit. Yes, I had to learn new technical skills but the way I used them was guided by my strengths.

When I had the chance to use my strengths, I crushed goals and assignments. When I couldn't use my *"toolkit"*, I struggled.

My Clifton StrengthsFinder results were:

1. **Deliberative:** Thinks thoroughly before acting.
2. **Connectedness:** Great at seeing how everything connects.
3. **Communication:** Easily converts an idea into words.
4. **Learner:** Obsession with learning something new.
5. **Individualization:** Passion for customizing and personalizing everything.

Here's a practical example.

In the vision chapter, I shared my idea to host a leadership seminar. Here's how I used my strengths:

- In setting the themes, I intentionally defined who I wanted to target and what I wanted them to get out of each training. *(Deliberative)*
- As I'm designing the courses, I thought about the participants and the jobs they had and then tailored my exercises and teachings based on my assumptions. *(Individualization)*
- I researched different training methods, read several articles and books, bounced ideas of volunteers, and ran a couple of surveys. *(Learner)*
- Educated myself about virtual meeting options, social media, video editing, and event planning best practices. *(Learner)*
- I purposely kept my teaching script straight forward and brief. *(Communication)*
- In developing the themes and finding speakers, I encouraged a similar theme and style of presentation. I

also created ways for all content to be housed in a single place so the participants didn't feel confused about where to go. *(Connectedness)*

There are three things I'd like to highlight in this example:

1. **Time-lapse.** The reason it took eight years to realize how my talents showed up in my daily activities was the lack of intentional reflection and application. It wasn't until I read the *"15 Invaluable Laws of Growth"* book that I understood the importance of purposeful action to transform talent into strengths.
2. **It takes practice.** By the time I hosted the leadership conference, I already had four years of refining the application of my strengths. Hence, I got quicker results because I knew what to focus on and what to delegate or ignore.
3. **Tests are only benchmarks not guarantees**. The StrengthsFinder test pointed to my areas of strengths but I still had to hone them to make them valuable. Tests can only point to the potential.

Let's Find Your Strengths

There are two ways I can share to start finding your strengths. They have different starting points but they follow a similar process.

Again, you pick the one that seems more appropriate to you at this moment and commit to testing it and making progress.

Remember, it's a journey of discovery. There are no prices to be won. No punishments for not getting excellent results right away. Permit yourself to play.

Option #1 - The Shortcut Assessment

I only share this method because it is the one I went through but don't feel pressured to follow it. Use it as a reference if you choose to go this route.

You can search the Internet for strengths assessments and find many variations in all price ranges.

As mentioned earlier, I had the opportunity to take the Clifton's StrengthsFinder test. You can buy the StrengthsFinder book that comes with a code to identify your top five strengths, or you can get a full report for $50 through Gallup's website. If you decide to purchase the book, make sure to get a new copy since the code can only be used once.

Again, since this method may incur an additional investment, I am not forcing you to use this method. I share it because it's what I did.

You can skip to *Option #2 – The Experiential Feedback Loop* if you are not planning on using this method.

I call it the shortcut assessment because many organizations have done the research and found a way to quickly present someone with their top five areas of strengths by using a questionnaire.

It shortens the time invested in trial and error using the experiential method in option #2.

I think of this process in two parts and applies to any type of assessment used:

1. Taking the assessment to set a benchmark and raise awareness

2. Intentional practice

Part #1 - Setting a benchmark and raising awareness

1. Take the assessment to get your top strengths.
2. Carve out the time to read the descriptions of each of your strengths.
3. Your focus for the first read-through is to understand what each name means.
   a. Seek to understand the definitions, first.
   b. Avoid figuring out how they apply to your life the first time you read about them.
   c. Seeking to agree or disagree will cause pre-judgment and will deter any opportunity for discovery and learning.
4. Now read the strength's descriptions a second time and create a list with the characteristics that align with the way you operate in the world.
5. Make a separate list with the characteristics that don't apply to you and save it for future reference.
6. Go back to the list of characteristics that align with you and reflect on your history and seek examples of you applying those strengths.
   a. For each example, think about the outcomes of those events.
   b. We are looking for data on relative success concerning your strengths.
7. Now, reflect on and create a list of any positive feedback received from others about something you did well
8. Take each item on the positive feedback list and consider the following:

a. How many of those positive moments were related to your use of the strengths?

b. Consider how natural it was for you to perform those activities.

c. We are looking for the relationship between positive outcomes and using your strengths.

9. If any of the lists is lacking or some strengths have no examples, that's okay. This is about having a point of reference.

Part #2 - Intentional Practice

This stage is where you get to internalize the results from your strengths assessment and validate what applies or not. This stage also helps to expand on the lists created in part one of the exercise. This part focuses on paying attention to the activities that come easy to you and create positive outcomes for you and others.

1. Start by picking one of your top strengths.

2. For the next seven days, set aside 5-10 minutes to reflect on the day's activities.

3. Here are five things you are looking for during your reflection time:

a. Activities relatively easy for you that other people regularly struggle with.

b. Activities you feel take a lot of energy and effort for you to complete.

c. Activities for which others praise you or come to you for advice.

d. Thinking patterns and ways you approached the day's tasks or problems.

e. Positive and negative highlights for the day.

4. What you are looking for are the places in which you used the strength you picked for the week.
   a. Feel free to review the description of the strength as you do the exercise.
   b. You may even want to read the description of the strength at the start of each day.
5. Continue this exercise for the seven days and note any consistent patterns.
6. Repeat these steps for each of your five strengths and cycle through it for as long as you want.

As you get used to the process, you'll be able to track multiple strengths daily.

The objective of this reflection exercise is to become intentional about looking for evidence of your strengths. Becoming aware of your strengths will help you implement the other steps of the *Greatness Within Framework*.

The more self-aware you are of your strengths, the easier it will be for you to prioritize what to focus on and what needs to be delegated or eliminated. I discuss prioritization in *Step #3: Purposely Claim Your Space.*

Option #2 - The Experiential Feedback Loop

This is the practical approach to discovering your strengths. It focuses on examining past experiences and trial and error to identify the areas in which you are gifted.

To structure your reflection time, I propose looking at your life from **three (3) core categories:**

1. **Natural Thinking Patterns:** while there is evidence we can change our thinking patterns, there seems to be a

natural bias in the ways we solve problems. For example, I look at problems from a bird's eye view before getting into the details. I don't just want to know the problem, I'd like to know how does it connect to everything else and how the pieces go together. This is part of my *connectedness* strength I mentioned in the prior exercise.

2. **Behaviors or Physical Aptitude:** this area is about any activity that comes easy to you or that you master very quickly.

3. **Specialized Skills:** whether physical, mental or technological these would be things you seem to be an expert in and that not everyone around you does well or they take a while to figure out.

This is a three-part process: identification, trial, and practice.

Part #1 - Identification Through Reflection

1. Set aside 15-30 minutes for reflection.

2. You can pick one of the core categories or approach it as a general reflection.

3. Create a list of responses as you consider these questions:

   a. What comes so naturally to you that you think everyone else does it but you are surprised when they tell you it was amazing?

   b. What are things you learned quickly with little effort?

   c. What are the activities you seem to have done well since the beginning?

   d. Recall memorable successes and identify common actions or behavioral patterns you applied.

e. What things do people come to you for advice or praise you for doing so well even though you think it's nothing out of the ordinary?

4. As you review your answers, look for common concepts. These are good candidates for natural strengths.

Part #2 - Let The Trial Begin

This is about validating your part #1 findings using feedback from other people.

1. Go to people you interact with often and ask them: When I am at my best, what do you see me do very well and with ease?

   a. Interview as many people as you can.

   b. Focus on getting specifics as it relates to activities, problem-solving skills, thinking processes, using tools, and technology.

   c. The objective is to have enough data to compare to your findings and discover things you didn't think about earlier.

2. Take the interview responses and identify common patterns

3. Compare notes with what you identified in part #1.

4. Any overlaps between part #1 and part #2 patterns serve as indicators of strengths.

5. For any new characteristics, consider running them through the *Identification Through Reflection* process.

Part #3 - Intentional Practice

This is similar to Part #2 of The Shortcut Assessment Option. But instead of using assessment results, you are using the patterns identified during your reflection time and interviews.

1. Start by picking one of your identified areas of strength from parts #1 and #2.
2. For the next seven days, set aside 5-10 minutes to reflect on the day's activities.
3. Here are four things you are looking for during your reflection time:
    a. In what ways did the strength show up throughout the day?
    b. What type of outcomes came up as a result of using your strength?
    c. What type of feedback did you get?
    d. What were your energy levels before and after using the chosen strength?
4. We are looking for evidence of what you do well with little effort and have a positive impact on your success.
5. Continue this exercise for the seven days and note any consistent patterns.
6. Repeat these steps for each of the possible areas of strength you have identified.

The more you reflect and the more data you gather, you'll increase your awareness of thought patterns, behaviors, and skills that come easy to you and help you succeed at what you do.

As with the prior exercises, give yourself permission to explore and go on a journey of discovery.

In the next chapter, we explore the last suit of courageously discovering your light. Similar to the vision chapter, I propose your next step to be taking the time to identify your strengths before we discuss **what gives flavor to everything you do.**

Chapter 7: The Values Suit – What Gives Flavor to Everything You Do

"People with different personalities, different approaches, and different values succeed not because one set of values or practices is superior, but because their values and practices are genuine."

~Herb Kelleher, former CEO of Southwest Airlines

The purpose suit identifies the filter through which we make all decisions. The vision suit describes the highest expression of our purpose. The strengths suit presents the tools we can use to make it all happen. And, **the values suit gives flavor to everything we do.**

I use the flavor analogy because others can have a similar purpose, vision, or talents but may not approach it the same way.

We know why we want something *(purpose)*. We know what we want *(vision)*. We know the tools we can use to make it happen *(strengths)*. What we need is a guidance system to apply it all. That's where values come into play.

Values set the standard for acceptable behaviors as we seek to thrive our way. Unfortunately, most people I meet aren't aware of their set of values.

What is non-negotiable in your life? What ideas or things would you give your life for?

I have discovered that when I have a strong positive or negative emotional reaction to a person, environment, or situation, it is directly related to alignment with my values. While I accept that life is more complex than ranking events based on a values checklist, being aware of my values has allowed me to properly analyze and learn from many emotionally charged experiences.

Here are four examples of this idea.

As a point of reference, my top five values are wisdom, courage, honesty, simplicity, and family.

Example #1: Political correctness makes everything worse

I believe political correctness loses its original intent when people use it to make everyone happy and to appear respectful and inclusive.

No. I am not advocating being condescending or insulting. I am referring to assuming that more neutral words are the solution.

Unfortunately, by beautifying words and making sure everything is neutral, it doubles or triples the time it takes to get the message across. Especially if they are delicate subjects because people start using ambiguous words and tiptoe around the topic trying to avoid any argument or miscommunication. In using neutral and polite wording, the statements can be watered down and the participants leave with completely different understanding of what was discussed.

Last time I checked, words only account for 7% or less of communication.

I dislike political correctness because it increases the complexity of communication *(Simplicity)*, and gives way to no one saying what they truly think *(Honesty)*.

Example #2: The truth will set you free

Born and raised by a father who had no hesitation in telling people what he thought, I learned to value sharing my thoughts and staying true to my beliefs.

Unfortunately, being direct with my words opens the door for misunderstandings and negative reactions due to taking things out of context.

It takes a level of courage and self-confidence to honor your beliefs regardless of how others may react to it.

This approach is directly related to me valuing *honesty & courage*. It's about the willingness to say it as I see it; and the courage to deal with the consequences of my words and actions.

Example #3: A few deep relationships are better than a plethora of acquaintances

I prefer quality time with close friends and loved ones. This is tied to me valuing *family*.

I enjoy investing time with those who I consider close friends. I prefer sharing life with a small inner circle of people than being the center of the party with a list of hundreds of connections.

The value of *family* is not just about the blood connection but also to those who I care for and consider important in my life. For them, I always have time and energy to help.

Example #4: I don't have time for chit-chatting
I have a strong dislike for people who aren't thoughtful enough in what they say and do. This is an expression of my *wisdom* value. These people say things like

- This is the way we have always done it.
- I do it just because.
- It's what everyone else does.
- Because I said so.
- Just tell me how to do it.

I value individuals who take their time to learn about a subject, are thoughtful with their actions, and invest time to find a solution to their issues.

It's about being intentional with their life as opposed to mimicking whatever everyone else is doing.

Three Considerations When Identifying Your Values

The previous four examples are a few ways my values affect what I do and how I interact with others.

You may have similar reactions to the same situations but may see it from a different angle based on what is non-negotiable to you.

The goal is to identify what you value in your life so you can make decisions based on what you value instead of what other people tell you is important.

Before going into the two exercises to help you identify your values, I wanted to share three (3) considerations to help you on your journey.

Consideration #1 - You Don't Have to Value What Society Says You Should

It's almost a cliché for people to say they value family first. As you can see from my results, that's not necessarily true.

Family does make my top five but it is not a requirement. Society tends to value things that don't apply to everyone.

As you go through the self-reflection process, avoid approaching it from the *"I should..."* mentality. The mentality that succumbs to peer pressure and trying to please and meet other people's expectations of you.

Consideration #2 - It's Not A Grading Exercise

School taught us to look at life with a grading framework. We study the ratings as if a person's individuality could be placed on a scale from 1 to 10.

As you go through the exercises and rank your values, it is not to be thought of as a rating scale but more as a priority system that helps you determine which values carry more weight in your decision-making process.

The difference between positions 1 and 5 could be minimal.

Also, just because other items don't make your top five doesn't mean they aren't important to you. It simply means they come after other things are addressed.

For example, when my wife identified her values, *"family"* was her first value. She wasn't happy with me placing family in fifth place. She thought 5th place meant the last place when in practice I treat my family as equally important as the other four.

The way the values priority applies to me means that I would take care of my family but I wouldn't do it at the expense of being honest with myself, thoughtful, and simple in my way of being.

Consideration #3 - Your Top Values Can Change as You Mature

In contrast to your purpose statement, your values may move places depending on the ebbs and flows of life.

While it may appear that your purpose statement changes, it is a variation caused by increased awareness and refinement of the statement. When it comes to what's non-negotiable, some items may move up or down the list based on life-changing events like the birth of a first child, getting married, losing a lost one to cancer, turning 50 years old, etc.

Let's get to exploring your values. You get to pick one of the two following exercises or do them both.

- The I-Beam, and/or
- The 5-Minute Discard Method

The I-Beam to Cross The Grand Canyon

I heard of this exercise while watching a seminar by Stephen R. Covey, the author of *"The 7 Habits of Highly Effective People"*.

This is a visualization exercise to discover what is non-negotiable in your life.

The process:

Suppose you are presented with a proposition. In front of you, there's a 100-foot I-Beam.

Side note: And I-Beam is usually made of structural steel, looks like a capital "I" or "H", and they are used in the foundations of civil engineering work.

The beam is about four inches off the ground. You stand on one end and I am on the other.

I then ask, "Would you walk across the beam for $100?"

Now, suppose the beam is about 10 floors high. Would you cross the beam for $100? What about $1,000? What about $50,000?

Let's take it up a notch.

Suppose the beam is still 10 floors high, but it's raining and slippery. How much would I have to give you for you to cross the beam in 2-minutes or less?

Here's the final scenario...suppose the beam now goes across the narrowest part of the Grand Canyon. It's about 600 feet long. That's a little over 1.5 football field lengths.

Freezing rain is coming down. The beam is about one mile high and it's about 12 inches wide. It's also windy.

Would you cross the beam from $1,000,000? Would you cross it if I had your child or loved one under threat of taking their life if you don't cross the beam?

The I-Beam exercise can quickly point out the importance of money versus family. But it can also identify what's important to you.

The key question is: in the last scenario, for what would you cross the I-Beam no matter the cost even if your life is at risk?

Brainstorm your answers and pay attention to what comes up. There's no right or wrong answer. Whatever you come up with has nothing to do with you being a good person or not. The exercise is purely helping identify what matters to you.

The list of answers helps you identify what's non-negotiable in your life and a starting point for testing what aligns with you and what doesn't.

The 5-Minute Discard Method

This is the method I used as instructed by John Maxwell's book, *"The 5 Levels of Leadership."*

This exercise is available all over the Internet so I just want to share a few pointers before you go through with it.

It's instinct, not logic
Each person experiences instinctual answers in different forms. Whether it's a feeling in a certain area of your body, sounds, or a specific type of thought, be open to following your instincts during this exercise.

It shouldn't take longer than five minutes to get your top five. But don't worry if it takes longer.

If you read a keyword and you have to think about it, that's probably a no. The objective is to select the ones that are an immediate "Yes."

There's no need for mathematical analysis or pro/cons lists.

If you insist on using a rating system, let's say on a scale of 1 to 10 you are looking for your 9s and 10s. Anything else will go to the "No" pile.

The process:

When I went through this process, I had printed cards with each word but feel free to come up with your way to do it.

Here are a few options to try:

- You can create your cards with each value on the list below.
- You can print the page or make a copy and scratch or circle your selections.
- You can go through the list and write down only the "Yes" on a piece of paper.

Regardless of which medium you use, the process is the same.

The Printed Cards Method

1. Without overthinking it, split the cards into a "Yes" or "No" pile.
2. After the first pass, pick the "Yes" pile and go through the process again.
    a. This time you are looking for absolutely "Yes."
    b. These are the words you immediately have a strong emotional connection to.
3. Keep going through the list until you have your top five.
4. To take it a step further, try to rank your top five.

The Scratch off Method

1. Print the list of values, make a copy, scan the page, or digitize it.

2. Without overthinking it, go through the list to circle the "Yes" and scratch off the "No or Maybe."
3. After the first pass, you will take circled words and scratch off the ones that aren't an absolute "Yes"
4. Keep going through the list until you have your top five.
5. To take it to the next level, try ranking your top five.

The paper can get messy as you go through the process. You may use different colored pens or create a new list with only the circled words. It's your choice.

The Write It Down Method

1. Choose your writing or typing medium.
2. Without overthinking it, go through the list and write down the values that are a definite "Yes"
3. After the first pass, look at the list and create a new list with only the ones that are an unquestionable "Yes."
4. Repeat the process until you have a list of five values.
5. To memorialize it, try ranking your top five values.

Feel free to combine methods. You know the objective and that's what matters.

List of Values I Used			
Quality	Commitment	Status	Passion
Trust	Legacy	Balance	Knowledge
Customer Satisfaction	Fitness	Achievement	Integrity
Perfection	Authority	Fairness	Growth
Diversity	Structure	Faith / Religion	Simplicity
Volunteerism / Service	Urgency	Independence	Family

Creativity / Innovation	Effectiveness	Loyalty	Honesty
Accountable	Recognition	Change	Wisdom
Fun	Money / Wealth	Competence	Courage
Teamwork	Efficiency		

I Have My Answers, What's Next?

Step #2 of the Greatness Within Framework, Courageously Discover Your Light, is probably the most involved because it requires plenty of time in self-reflection and exploration.

The time and effort invested is worth it because it sets the foundation for your independence from other people's agendas and the path to stop seeking validation.

I don't know about you but I have spent too many years seeking ways to fit in. I have tried so many things to get people to understand where I come from, to listen to what I share, and to welcome me into their circles. I have given too much of my life force to molding myself to meet society's expectations to belong.

It's such a common practice that we tend to think it's the right thing to do. Yet, if we can agree that each person is different. And, each of us can have a unique perspective, *how can a group of people know more about what's best for us if they all have different perceptions of reality?*

If we morph to fit someone else's view of who we should be, this leaves us at the mercy of someone else's preferences and agenda. We wouldn't have full autonomy in our lives.

Hence, to create a life worthy of us, we must first identify what drives us to do great things, what would be the ideal life, what do we stand for, and how we can build it.

We must know ourselves well to have an independent point of reference as we seek to thrive our own way.

The next steps of the *Greatness Within Framework* are about implementation and dealing with the challenges that inevitably show up when you reinvent yourself.

- Purposely claiming your space,
- Confidently filtering the critics, and
- Gratefully welcome the journey.

Before moving on, remember this is an iterative process. The more you increase your self-awareness and refine your answers, the simpler it is to go through life minding your business immune to what others think of you. Stay the course and allow yourself to discover.

Chapter 8: Preparing For The Road Less Traveled

Every time you are tempted to react in the same old way, ask if you want to be a prisoner of the past or a pioneer of the future.

~Deepak Chopra

Let's take a moment to appreciate what has been done so far.

Something I don't do well is acknowledge small wins and the progress made. I invite you to take a few moments and review what you have done up until now.

The journey started by recognizing that it is still possible to fail while following society's best practices and the experts' best advice regardless of their well-meaning intentions.

Such a revelation can leave you feeling lost, out of place, and wondering what's next.

But you chose to hit the reset button and create life your way. After all, *if you can follow best practices and fail, why not just follow what you want to do and see what happens?*

Thus, you went through **Step #1** of the *Greatness Within Framework*, **Passionately Challenge Everything You Know** about yourself.

You have challenged the labels, looks, behaviors, and thoughts that appear to define you in order to make room for who you are meant to be. You took the hand you were dealt, and asked for a new one.

The next step was to figure out the new hand by courageously entering the process of identifying…

- Why you are here *(Purpose)*
- What you want your life to be *(Vision)*
- What can you use to create this new life *(Strengths)*, and
- What's non-negotiable in your life (Values)

These four areas form the four suits of **Step #2** *of the Greatness Within Framework,* **Courageously Discover Your Light.**

Regardless of how robust are your findings and answers, you now have a benchmark to start letting go of seeking validation and create a life that is worthy of you.

Which brings us to the next step of the *Greatness Within Framework.*

Step #3 - Purposely Claiming Your Space

This is where we transform our thinking from the previous steps in the framework into practical implementation steps. This is where life starts getting aligned to who we are and who we want to become.

What do I mean by purposely claiming your space?

I'll start with the word *"purposely"*.

Creating a life worthy of us demands intentionality. No one else has it on their agenda to build our ideal life for us.

The journey also requires purposeful action because, if we don't pay attention, life has a way of filling in the gaps with whatever is the next urgency.

There's always someone wanting something from us, an emergency shows up, something breaks in the house, a fire drill at work, etc.

If we don't pay attention, we get lost in the busyness of life and forget about our original vision to create a life we are excited to wake up to.

When it comes to *"claiming your space,"* an analogy that comes to mind is when animals pee around the perimeter to set their territory so they can move freely within a certain area.

Thus, one way to claim our space is to figure out a way to set boundaries.

It's like a buffer of mental and physical space to ensure that whatever we interact with is in alignment with where we want to go and who we are becoming.

Claiming your space is declaring your intent to others and the universe by using your answers from Step #2 of the framework as the benchmark.

The Price to Be Paid to Claim Your Space

I have to admit that everything I'm sharing with you in this book is stuff I figured out in hindsight.

When I started my journey, I had no idea where I was going. I had no idea who to talk to. I didn't have a vision, a purpose statement, identified values, or knew my strengths.

It was all new, overwhelming and uncomfortable.

My family, friends, and coworkers all knew and expected me to be a certain way. But I was taking a different route and changing things altogether.

As expected, the change wasn't received with open arms. To them I was supposed to be a certain person, doing things a certain way and incapable of doing something else.

The lack of reception combined with the stress of not knowing what to do gave way to doubt and worry.

- Will they still like me?
- What's going to happen to my career?
- What will my parents think?
- Will I still have friends?
- What if I lose my job?
- What if I fail?
- Can I really do this?
- What's the best way to start?

To figure it out, I first had to ask myself if the journey was worth the expected criticism, letting go of relationships, switching jobs, and saying goodbye to the habits that got me to the level of success I had until that moment.

This is a valid question to ask yourself and it shouldn't be taken lightly.

It wasn't fun to feel like I was alone on an island. It hurt when I shared a passionate idea to a friend and they brushed it off as daydreaming. It wasn't easy to have my spouse be against the new direction and advocating, like everyone else, to stay in my *"financially secured"* job.

The decision to bet on myself was simple but difficult.

A Simple Process For Claiming Your Space

Like any other beginner, armed with my notes from the exercises in *Step #2 of the Greatness Within Framework,* I looked for the tools and strategies proposed by different leadership and personal development experts to determine how to create a life worthy of me.

I explored tools like goal setting, priority management, time management techniques, developing a support system, etc.

The techniques are easy to find and test. But they felt like band-aids dressing superficial wounds because the ***true change came from going within.***

I realized that while external actions can create habits that change the way we look at things, I had to look closely at the internal beliefs that prevented me from taking consistent action.

There were ideas like wanting to be liked by everyone, getting it right the first time, and not wanting to show I didn't know what I was doing.

I also discovered that working through the mental barriers is a greater challenge but produces the greatest return. Hence, I speak first about the mental barriers, and then about the tools and techniques.

The Mental Barriers

1. Other People's Agendas (People Pleasing)
2. The Need To Get It Right (Perfectionism or Fear of Failure)
3. The Desire for Balance (Work/Life Balance)

The Practices

1. Filter The Noise: The Art of Pruning
2. A Fenced Playground is Better: Boundaries Create Freedom
3. Never Do It Alone But Not Everyone Should Be Invited
4. Reinvent Continuously: Success Demands Growth

This is not an extensive list. These are the things that work better for me and seek to apply daily.

Like the rest of the framework, approach it all with a learning mindset, test the concepts, refine, and adapt them to your style. Take what you need, and ignore the rest.

Chapter 9: The Biggest Obstacle To Thriving Your Way

"Until you make the unconscious conscious it will rule your life and you will call it fate."

~Carl Jung

Anyone can share resources with the *"X Tips to Cure [insert problem]"* but few people take time to discuss the mental aspect of the game.

The next three chapters discuss the three mental barriers I needed to conquer when *applying Step #3 - Purposely Claim Your Space.*

As a refresher, the three barriers are:

1. Other People's Agendas *(People Pleasing)*
2. The Need To Get It Right (Perfectionism or Fear of Failure)
3. The Desire for Balance (Work/Life Balance is a Scam)

Let's begin.

Mental Barrier #1: Other People's Agendas

If you asked people who have observed my life's journey, they would likely consider me an independent person.

I thought the same until I noticed how focused I was on meeting other people's expectations. As evidenced by the three memories I shared earlier in chapter 1.

Back in 2004, thanks to changes in medical coverage regulations and company growth, I ended up in a role where:

- My work directly affected the financial metrics of the company.
- I had to become an expert in something everyone was doing for the first time.
- I had to explain actuarial concepts to people of different educational backgrounds. And,
- I was learning and being challenged daily.
- It was great. I felt important.

Over time, I got better at many things. With the expertise came promotions and more responsibilities. *I climbed the ladder of success.*

I climbed until I suffered from what is known as **"the paradox of success."** A process I can describe in four statements:

1. I became successful.
2. My success attracted more projects.
3. I liked the attention and said yes to everything.
4. I was responsible for so many things I burned out and failed.

My problem came from believing and wanting to do it all so I could help and be liked by everyone.

*I let the need to feel important transform me
into a people pleaser.*

- I hid the people pleasing mentality by thinking:
- I like helping others.
- I must help my customers get what they need.
- I need to resolve what my market leaders ask for.
- I need to fix it because I'm the expert and I can do it faster.
- Or the classic, "But they need me to…"

All these phrases are acceptable in moderation but my problem was that I used them 24/7.

With repetition, I came to believe them. And as soon as I believed them, I constantly looked for evidence that people valued my work. If I didn't see enough evidence, I got angry.

I said things like:

- They don't pay me enough for this.
- No one listens to me.
- I'm the only one that cares.
- Must be nice to leave at five every day.
- Why do I have to fix everything?

I said all these things because I believed that my sole purpose was to make sure everyone got what they needed, except myself.

I forgot the wisdom of the classic phrase "you cannot give what you do not have." Sooner or later, the tank goes empty.

Whether you consider yourself a people pleaser or not, consider the following question:

In what ways have you allowed your actions to be influenced by fear of what other people may think of you or the obligation to meet their expectations?

The people pleaser mindset's signs are subtle. They are usually a couple of layers deep in our thinking patterns.

I use the three memories from chapter one as examples.

I agreed to play baseball because my father spent years telling me I needed to play a sport. I started with Shotokan Karate, then basketball, soccer, and finally baseball. I stayed with baseball because I noticed I had some talent. I was good enough to keep going. But behind it all, my deepest reason for practicing the sport was because I thought that was the way my father would be proud of me and keep loving me.

I knew his dedication to taking me wherever I needed to go to play. The daily practices, the weekend tournaments, the purchase of equipment, the special batting classes, the athletic tests, etc. I saw him giving his time, money, and effort to take me places. I believed the best I could do to honor him was to keep playing.

I became an actuary because my mother suggested it. Also, it was different and fully aligned with my father's reprimand, *"do you really want to be like everyone else?"*

My mom was there for me, too. She took care of school activities, the clothing, the meals, the social events, and supported me in the baseball tournaments. I felt a sense of obligation to do the best I could to make her actions worthwhile. I trusted her, so I just thought what she said was a good idea.

As for my corporate career, my focus was to help the best I could. I followed the societal advice to show up early, leave late, and get it done. Also, I understood that I needed to be politically correct, follow direction, and fit in because that was how to be promoted and continue to help others. I was trying to find my place in the world; thus, I felt a need to comply and play within the rules because that's what was working for others.

Notice the deeper reasons behind my actions. While there is positive intent, it is also highly driven by fear of failure or an obligation to meet someone else's expectation besides my purpose to help others and make a difference.

By no means I am saying these actions are wrong or that one should ignore others' advice. These are examples of how the *people pleasing* mindset sneaks into our way of living.

I consider this mindset the biggest obstacle to thriving your way because as you claim your space you'll inevitably do and say things that some people in your current circles of influence will not approve of. And the key to success lies in your willingness to let these people's expectations have no hold on you.

Five Considerations to Let Go of The People Pleasing Mindset?

Claiming independence from other's expectations of you requires a deeper recognition of what's behind this need to make other people happy.

As I reflect on my life and why I let other people's opinions and expectations have so much weight in what I did, it *all comes down to seeking validation to find a place to fit in, a place to belong*. An environment where I don't have to worry about what I say and do because someone could take offense.

It's interesting to see life be distilled into such a simple concept. It all comes down to survival and tribal mentality.

Some say that in the early stages of human civilization, human survival depended on being part of the tribe. Each person had their role and understood that being expelled from the community tremendously increased the chances of death.

Also, it seems natural to want to be part of a group or community. This bias to feel connected to someone else even if it is just two strangers from the same country running into each other while vacationing on the same foreign land.

Whether one is introverted or extroverted, it looks like humans seek for a group to fit in.

All the people pleasing I have done can be boiled down to wanting to belong.

Why should this need to belong matter to let go of the people pleasing?

Because once it is acknowledged it can be addressed.

In recognizing this inherent need to belong we now have the power to consciously choose where to belong instead of trying to satisfy it by forcing ourselves to fit wherever we are.

I cannot recall the specific moment when I recognized that my work environment was not a fit but I do remember the switch in awareness.

Before the insight, I was constantly stressed and disappointed with anything related to work. I felt misunderstood, devalued, and out of place. For years, I tried hard to get others to receive my ideas but rarely did I succeed. It was like I was talking in a different language. The harder I tried to fit in the more frustrated I got. It reached the point where I thought it was my fault.

Then, one day, I finally accepted that it wasn't anyone's fault or problem. It simply wasn't a match. The people I interacted with daily were simply on a different wavelength and it was like trying to mix oil and water. I could adapt for short periods but I would break down, eventually. **I was tolerated not appreciated.**

What helped me realize the misfit was a weekly leadership symposium I facilitated the last three years of my tenure in that company. Over time, the same words and communication style was producing opposite reactions in the symposium as compared to my coworkers.

I thought to myself, "how is it possible that I feel so much more comfortable in the weekly discussions than with the people I work with daily?"

At first glance, I could say it was different people with different backgrounds and values. But, at a deeper level, it was the difference between creating my path and being assigned to one.

I was assigned to work in my department. I didn't play a part in deciding who would work in it. With the leadership symposium, I simply invited people to participate and through my facilitation style, people voluntarily kept coming or not.

Don't miss the point. *The difference came from charting my course and letting the pieces come together.*

I went from trying to fit in whichever environment I was to creating my way and give others the opportunity to join or not.

Transitioning away from forcing myself to belong is an ongoing process for me.

I submit to you five considerations to break away from forcing yourself to fit in the categories other people expect, demand, or want you to fit in.

A. Separate Identity from Outcomes
"What do you want to be when you grow up?"

A question any child answers with boundless imagination.

As the child grows, the answers lose their intensity and are replaced with goals to achieve certain grades, obtain a college degree, a financially secure job, and other accolades.

The change is not sudden but the outcome of a societal and educational system programmed to shift focus from the greatness within to having our careers, achievements, and possessions define us.

Maybe your experience was similar to:

- Parents and the educational system make you believe that to amount to something we must have a respectable profession
- To get such a job we must have a degree from a reputable university
- To get accepted to this university one needs excellent grades and impressive extracurricular activities

- Since the parents want the best for their children, they frequently remind the children to stay in school and keep high grades.
- If a low grade appears in the report, immediate interrogation ensues, some version of punishment is applied, and actions are taken to ensure that the grade improves the next time.
- Since getting good grades becomes such an important thing to parents, the child makes the connection that to do well and be loved by others it is necessary to have good grades.
- Failing to get good grades implies not getting to a prestigious university, thus eliminating the option to succeed and be valuable to the world.

In short, the "WHO" is replaced with a "WHAT."

Thus, we spend most of our early life worrying about this question: What does it say about me if I cannot meet other people's expectations of me?"

The first belief to break is that the **"WHAT's"** in our lives define who we are.

For us to create a life that is worthy of us, we must be okay with taking actions independently of what other people expect from us or think about our actions.

B. Love Doesn't Need Proof

I think we all want to make our parents proud. We have an instinct to want to be loved by our parents. Thus, we do what they tell us to do. Their opinions have a significant impact on our life choices. And, we seek to make them happy. We believe that if we do what pleases them, then we would continue to be loved.

Interestingly, my daughter has proven me wrong on this matter. With her natural way of being she has shown me the true meaning of love.

Before I welcomed a daughter to this world, I found it fascinating how almost every friend's gathering conversation was dominated by stories of their children.

I couldn't understand it back then, but I can now.

The moment I saw my daughter's birth, I felt something that words cannot describe. A feeling that changed my perspective on life and what it means to live.

In an instant, nothing else mattered but taking care of the newborn.

As time has passed and she grows, I am constantly reminded that no matter the chaos, no matter what she does, that feeling doesn't go away.

My love for her transcends the physical world. Actions taken by my daughter don't affect how much I love her.

Will I feel anger, disappointment, or frustration? Absolutely. But, as they say, love for a child is unmovable.

If this feeling is commonly felt by parents around the world, I have to wonder why did I spend so much time trying to make my parents proud?

Regardless of the answer, there's enough experiential evidence to accept that I don't need to force myself to live a life according to what my parents want to be loved.

Hence, it is okay to chart a new course.

C. Friends Make You Better Not Hold You Back

Friends become the first space outside our home where we want to fit in. We value what they say and we want to make them feel good.

Unfortunately, this can also create a scenario in which we hold ourselves back because we worry about what our friends may think or that we could grow apart.

While there's nothing wrong with wanting to belong, keep it in perspective.

I believe there's a common misconception about friendships.

The idea that friends should accept you just the way you are is incomplete. Especially, where one person has a destructive habit.

A friend is one who participates in the journey of helping you become a fuller expression of yourself.

This requires not only acceptance of where you are at this specific point with no strings attached but, also, a desire to help you be, do, and have a life worthy of you.

There's a difference between wanting someone to be exactly how I believe they should be and wanting them to be the best they can be.

A friend aids in our transformation from a hesitant follower to a confident creator of our lives.

A friend keeps us from destroying ourselves. A friend supports our journey without needing us to be a certain way.

> *"No person is your friend who demands your silence, or denies your right to grow."*
>
> ~*Alice Walker*

D. Working Together Doesn't Mean Doing It The Same Way

I remember the moment I stopped pursuing becoming a Fellow of the Society of Actuaries.

To most of my fellow Actuarial peers, that was career suicide because high-level promotions in my profession required that level of certification.

As a matter of reference, it is similar to only getting an associate versus a bachelor's degree.

As expected, several of my peers who finished their fellowship got promoted shortly after they got it.

We all had the same responsibilities but I made much less money than them.

It hurt. It made me doubt myself. It gave me the fear of missing out.

- What have I done?
- Will I ever get a promotion?
- Is this really it?
- Am I not good enough?
- Am I being left behind?

The negative self-talk came with my peers reinforcing that I "needed" to finish the exams so I could be considered valuable to the business.

I took about a year to make peace with the decision.

A short time later, I was promoted to a role equivalent in pay as if I had finished my fellowship certification. It took longer than others but it proved that I didn't commit career suicide.

Furthermore, I noticed that several actuarial vice-presidents didn't have their fellowship certification either.

There can be many roads to the same destination.

I believe what matters is that we pick the one that's in alignment with our way of life.

E. You Are The Measuring Stick

I'd like to propose a mental exercise.

Suppose people pleasing is necessary. That for us to belong, we must fit into whichever social circle we are a part of by meeting other people's expectations of who we *should be*.

Consider the implications of meeting the demands of such a scenario. It's meeting the demands from parents, friends, family, coworkers, and society in general.

Then, add the expectations from the plethora of groups one can be a member of. The religion, political affiliation, economic status, age groups, etc.

Let's say that by some miraculous process we do manage to meet every single one of those requirements.

By the assumption of this scenario, we have succeeded. But there's one major flaw.

No one, except for us, has enough data, perspective, and understanding to know who we are.

Others can help us improve but they can't have the entire picture.

Thus, even if we succeed and meet all those expectations, all we would be doing is becoming a version of ourselves determined by people who have incomplete data.

And, if we aren't truly ourselves, are we truly belonging?

You are the only one that can determine whether life fully aligns with who you are.

So, there you have it, five considerations to break the people pleasing habit:

    A. Separate identity from outcome
    B. Love doesn't need proof
    C. Friends make you better not old you back
    D. Working together doesn't mean doing it the same way
    E. You are the measuring stick

Before moving on to the next mental barrier take a few minutes to ponder on these five ideas and the question I asked earlier in the chapter:

> *In what ways have you allowed your actions to be influenced by fear of what other people may think of you or the obligation to meet their expectations?*

Chapter 10: Don't Let Step #2 Stop You From Taking Step #1

Perfectionism is a distraction, a justification for procrastination, an excuse for never getting anything done. It's a refusal to accept reality, and it is rooted in fear. To the perfectionist, nothing will ever be good enough.

~Dr. Henry Cloud

The mind dislikes the unknown. It likens it to risk getting attacked by a panther in the middle of the night. Call it the *lizard brain* or *survival instinct* but it definitely spends a lot of energy figuring out possible threats so it can prepare accordingly.

It doesn't help that the education system programs us to believe failure is guaranteed if we don't answer correctly.

This mentality of *"needing"* to get it right easily transfers into adulthood. For example:

- It's keeping quiet instead of asking for clarification to avoid sounding stupid.
- It's delaying making a decision with partial information to avoid making a mistake.
- It's holding off on taking action until there's a detailed project plan in place that's been approved by all department leaders.
- It's avoiding a new activity for fear of looking silly.
- It's keeping the *"safe"* job because it's familiar.

Welcomed to the next mental barrier to **purposely claiming your space**…

Mental Barrier #2: The Need to Get It Right

My father raised me to always be looking for ways to improve things. He also scolded me by using the question "do you want to be like everybody else?" To remind me that to stand out one must do things right or not do them at all.

This upbringing combined with my strengths of deliberative, connectedness, and individualization created a strong bias towards perfectionism.

This nurturing was reinforced by my actuarial science studies since we were expected to produce accurate financial projections.

To give some context to this need for accuracy, I estimated member premiums for a block of business with 366,000 members.

The average monthly premium for the block was about $900 per member per month.

A 1% error margin, or a 99% accuracy, meant a $9 plus or minus window. If I missed the projections by $9, it meant a $9 x 366,000 x 12 = $39,528,000 mistake.

I remember a year where I made a $20 million mistake. My superiors weren't too happy about it.

This is just one of the many ways *the need to get it right* has been reinforced in my professional career but it also expands into my personal life.

When I decided to stop seeking validation and create a life worthy of me, I was launching into something I had never done before.

Thus, to have some sense of control, I applied what I had done for decades...research, study, develop models, and try to get it right the first time.

My mind was doing everything possible to avoid feeling like I felt that day in the break room.

Here are several things I did before taking meaningful action:

- Jumped from webinar to webinar collecting the "next best practices"
- Spent days researching the best way to set goals
- Collected Personality assessments
- Went through 73 books and audiobooks in six months as preparation
- Spent weeks or months planning and *"thinking"* about a specific project idea
- Shared my ideas with anyone willing to listen to validate them

I don't know if this is something you experience but I regularly catch myself preparing to prepare and delaying execution all because I want the most efficient way to do something the right way just to discover adjustments have to be made as soon as I act on the idea.

Some personalities are very good at starting and adjusting on the fly, but if you try to get it right before you move remember this...

You don't have to be great to start, but you have to start to be great.

~Zig Ziglar

Let me share with you three thoughts that have helped me come to peace with launching imperfectly.

#1 - Progress Not Perfection: It's Easier to Be Right The More Outcomes You Have

I laugh at this one because it's an accepted statistical fact that the more data points we have, the easier it is to adjust and predict future outcomes.

But my mind fights to plan things thoroughly and not take the first step if I cannot see step #4 or 10 working properly.

My connectedness strength helps me see the bigger picture. My individualization strength likes to personalize experiences for people. My deliberative strength seeks for the pros and cons of things and thoroughly examines the possible paths forward.

It shouldn't be a surprise that when I get an idea, I tend to not want to start until I have every single "how-to" figured out and certain that it can work.

The problem is that my big picture thinking can get so big that, for me to launch, it would take months of focused work to get it all figured out.

Hence, my virtual workbench is filled with dozens of projects I started but never finished because figuring out the execution of the big picture became overwhelming.

How effective can I be if I only try something once and don't get the expected outcome?

How feasible is it to succeed if I take several months to just take the first step to something I have never done before?

In switching from following other people's advice to figuring out what you want your life to be there will be a lot of *"firsts."*

You could read the car driver's manual but there's no way you'll know how to drive unless you are actually behind the wheel in a moving car.

And even if you pass your driver's test, some people will not trust you to be a good driver. But the more you drive, the greater the variety of experiences you have to adjust your technique until you become a master driver.

When I was first learning to drive a manual transmission car, it took all my focus and energy to figure out how to shift gears.

One day, I was driving on a busy road. As I neared a curve, I accidentally shifted into 4th gear instead of 2nd.

To correct my mistake, I looked down to the gearbox to remind myself of the location of the 2nd gear. I didn't notice when the car veered into oncoming traffic and I almost crashed into a car.

If it wasn't for the instructor who quickly pulled on the wheel and triggered the emergency brakes, it would have been a nasty experience.

In time, and with repetition, I got to where I didn't need to think about it.

I had memorized the driver's manual. I have had hundreds of hours with car racing video games and simulations, but nothing could replace driving a car.

The more I drove the car, the better I got and the easier it was to figure out how the car moved, how it felt in certain situations, and how to deal with other cars on the road.

It was progress, not perfection that got me to be a relative expert driver.

Regardless of how much of a challenge this is for you, I relay this statement I heard some time ago: *it's easier to steer a car when it's moving than when it's parked.*

#2 - What Doesn't Kill You Makes You Stronger: The Willingness to Be Wrong

The prior thought was a logical approach. This one I consider emotional.

This is about the fear of failure.

I have the type of personality that doesn't like to be wrong. I am thoughtful and thorough with my planning because I don't like to make mistakes and be criticized for them.

It's an interesting situation because I also like to learn and make mistakes as part of the learning process.

I guess I am okay when I make mistakes and no one else is involved. But if someone else could be affected by it or depends on what I am doing, then I have a problem with making mistakes.

I connect it with my purpose.

If I want to help others discover their capacity to create a life worthy of them, I must show I know what I am talking about. If I make mistakes or fail, people won't want to listen. If they don't listen then I won't be able to fulfill my purpose. And, so on.

I believe the fear of failure expresses the idea that I must be useful to society to avoid being cast away and *"die alone."*

When it comes down to it, ***the only solution that has helped me take the next step forward and be willing to be wrong is getting to a "nothing to lose" or "I'm learning something" mentality.***

The "nothing to lose" mentality is related to my epiphany in the break room: *if I can fail following other people's best advice, I might as well try building a life my way. If I fail, I'm back where I started. But if I succeed, I have a life that excites me.*

The *"I'm learning something"* mentality is to consider all steps taken as another outcome collected that I can use to make progress and *"steer the car"* towards my destination.

This mindset shift recognizes that getting to the end of the line with a bunch of "what ifs" is much more painful than the mistakes that can happen along the way towards creating a life worthy of me.

Ultimately, the willingness to be wrong requires one to...

#3 - Reconnect With Your Fearless Inner Child: The Beauty Of Discovery

Being a father has reminded me of how simple was life before adult responsibilities came into my life.

There's something about the innocence of a child that brings forth the best of human nature: **the passion for learning and discovery.**

It only takes a few minutes of observing a child interact with the world to realize that they have no filter.

If they see something of interest, they touch, grab, shake, or throw it.

If they want something, they just go get it.

When they climb something, it doesn't even register that they can fall until they do. Then get up and try again.

To them, the world is a playground and it is out there for them to engage with and learn from it.

Some have said that we are born with only two fears: the fear of loud noises and the fear of quick changes in altitude (falling).

If that is true, where does the need to be right every time come from?

I think it is in our nature to be fearless in pursuing learning and mold the world to support our evolution.

Reconnecting with the inner child is not about thinking of unicorns and rainbows but approaching life intending to play and discover ways to express ourselves in the world.

I find this concept difficult to implement.

I have bills to pay, a job to maintain, money to be made, a house to take care of, a family to feed, and all those things "adults" are supposed to manage.

Yet, the moments when I am at my best are the ones where I am just being myself, enjoying the experience, the people I am with, and the work that's getting done. It feels a lot like play even when the stakes are high and mistakes can have major negative consequences.

By learning to see life as an opportunity to explore and have fun, I have been able to move forward even when I don't have every step figured out.

The best example that comes to mind is my experience doing leadership training in Paraguay.

I'm in Paraguay with 260 other coaches looking to make a difference under one simple motto:

We are going someplace, at some time, to meet someone, and do something.

I'm there excited and afraid. We are all in a room getting to know each other and receiving instructions. In the middle of it, Paul takes the stage to give an impromptu announcement.

We need 13 Spanish speaking coaches to travel overnight to unscheduled destinations, please come forward for a debrief!

I have no idea what took over me but I just stood up and walked to the front with determination. Yet, I couldn't ignore the voice in the back of my head saying: what in the world are you thinking Juan?

At any rate, I did it. I traveled four hours by car to work with a cooperative formed by families of German descent.

Go figure, my first time doing the training, and doing it for people with Spanish as their second language!

With that adventure finished, I got back to Asunción to continue with the "scheduled programming."

The way it worked was: You ate breakfast, you got in line, and someone came to pick you up, to take you someplace, at some time, to meet someone, and do something.

This time around, I got to visit the Paraguayan consulate.

As it happens often, things didn't go as planned. We took materials for a half-day worth of training and we quickly discovered we would be there all day. So, we had to figure how to make it work with what we had until the extra materials showed up.

I have no idea how but, somehow, I ended up leading the group and organizing the engagement.

I connected so well worth the organizer Diego, that I told him "I don't know how I'm going to do it, but I'll come back tomorrow"

I did go back and not only that, thanks to my connection with Diego and his staff, I got the chance to train their team of executives including a congresswoman.

What a great experience and adventure.

I was so excited at the moment I forgot to recognize the craziness of it all.

It wasn't until I was coming back to the US. That I realize the only thing that made it possible was my willingness to suspend the requirement of knowing how to do it and just have fun.

Am I consistently operating in this mindset? Not at all. But I know I can access that level of thinking and produce great results.

My encouragement to you?

Trick your mind to think of a major project as a game. Frame your mind to see it as a learning process rather than a destination that needs precise movements.

I'll end this portion with a simple question: *if you have never done it before, what makes you think that you'll know which way is the right way before you even start the journey?*

Recall the car analogy from earlier. Until you are doing it, there's no certain way for you to know if it will work or not. What works for one person may not work for you. It's your light, your world, your journey.

The latter is why I'm writing this with zero expectation of you doing what I have done. I'm simply sharing a framework to help you discover your way of creating a life worthy of you.

Chapter 11: Stop Spinning Plates

"It is the same with people as it is with riding a bike. Only when moving can one comfortably maintain one's balance."

~Albert Einstein

I used to believe in work-life balance and spent a lot of energy trying to achieve it.

Unfortunately, I was not ever successful.

I felt like a plate spinner trying to keep 10 plates balanced on their stick without ever taking a break.

Have you seen a plate-spinning act?

Have you noticed how stressful it can be?

It's an entertaining sketch but, in the end, no real progress is made. It takes a lot of effort to balance that many plates and keep them going without falling.

That's how I felt during the peak of my corporate career.

I wanted to keep everything in check.

Studying for exams, work projects, staff management responsibilities, social activities, exercise, family, friends, personal development, church activities, etc.

No matter how hard I tried, something always fell through the cracks.

And the rare moments when I felt life was balanced, I noticed no progress was being made.

Such is the irony of **mental barrier #3, the desire for balance.**

If we take an objective view, balance means nothing is pulling in any direction. It's static.

No progress can be made when everything in life is balanced.

A better approach is to replace balance with harmony, alignment, or seasons.

It's about having the different areas of life aligned in the same direction.

Let's use Einstein's bicycle analogy as an example.

Have you tried balancing on a bike in place?

It takes a lot of effort.

- Keeping the handles straight
- Holding the pedals still
- Balancing your body weight
- Adjusting your feet and legs to counteract the bike's movements.

Contrast it to how easy it is to maintain balance while you are riding the bicycle. All it takes is pedaling every so often and ensuring the handles keep the front wheel aligned in the direction you want to go.

What is interesting about this analogy is that the parts of the bike move at different speeds and timings.

- The gear attached to the pedals spins faster than the gear attached to the rear wheel.
- The wheels turn at a different speed than the pedals.
- The handlebar, body of the bike and you stay in position while the bicycle does most of the work.
- The breaks are only activated when you desire to do so.
- The tires just do their thing and are replaced after a certain amount of mileage.

Each piece is part of the entire journey and moves and works at a different pace but towards the same purpose.

That's the way life should be. Not balanced but aligned.

Like the seasons, certain areas of life will get more focus and time than others but they all point to the same destination.

What Does This Have to Do With Creating A Life Worthy Of You?

Learning to think in terms of harmony and alignment rather than balance is key to managing the emotional rollercoaster in the early stages of applying the *Greatness Within Framework.*

When my journey started, I recall feeling overwhelmed by all that needed to change after I stopped trying to meet other people's expectations and started doing my thing.

During the process of identifying what I loved, my purpose, my strengths, what I wanted to create, and with whom I wanted to invest my life force, I realized that a lot of my life had to change.

- The people I worked with didn't have the same interests.
- The "friends" I had were superficial relationships focused on hanging out rather than helping each other grow
- The department I worked for showed little support for personal development, and
- The work I was doing was financially great but lacked satisfaction and kept pulling me away from what I loved to do.

I noticed the activities I was in and the people around me were pulling me away from what I wanted and reinforced the need to play a certain persona.

The more I tried to make things fit, the more I felt out of place and out of *balance*.

What helped me find a sense of control was focusing on setting a vision for what I wanted, get to know myself well enough, be at peace with the difference, and fill in the gaps that the current circumstances of life weren't fulfilling.

I found my sense of alignment with blogging on leadership, engaging with fellow John Maxwell Team members, facilitating the leadership symposium, weightlifting, and playing baseball.

Over time, I shifted my focus to things, people, and places aligned with what I wanted to create. I couldn't do it all at once, and not everything got my full attention every day, but I made room to tend to them regularly.

Finding alignment will depend on the clarity of the outcomes from *Step #2 - Courageously Discover Your Light*.

Remember, this is a journey. It's a continual study of yourself and adjustments will have to be made as you progress.

A Final Thought on Balance

When it comes to creating a life that's a full expression of yourself, balance is a lie.

Balance is the lie the ego uses to keep us tied to the things society promotes.

It's connected to the mentality of scarcity.

- The early bird gets the worm.
- Hard work pays off.
- Life favors the early riser.
- There are only so many pieces of the pie.

These are only a few of the fancy phrases we like to repeat all the time while unconsciously reinforcing the idea that only the special unicorns can create a life in their own terms.

Balance is what I used to force myself to invest the same time in all areas of my life believing that without it I would not be happy. Thus, I continued to exhaust myself trying to achieve a work-life balance and then judged myself when I was spending too much time in entertainment instead of studying for exams or working out.

The irony of it all is that when I felt like I was balanced, I was emotionally spent and sensed something missing. I felt out of place. I felt like I was going in circles.

Balance is what I used to keep myself in a job I disliked, in a department that didn't value my skills, and hanging out with people who didn't have the same interests out of fear of being lonely.

Balance is the concept I used for decades to say no to myself and continue living undercover.

What opened my eyes to a new reality was the transformation trip to Paraguay. It was five days long and I probably slept 15 hours throughout the trip. Sixteen-hour days followed by networking. Yet, I loved every moment of it and was energized the entire trip.

Why?

Because I was doing what I loved, with people who valued each other's gifts and making an impact in other people's lives by using my talents.

There's no way I was balanced.

What I experienced was the alignment of all the pieces I discussed in Step #2.

What reinforced this finding was reflecting on all the times I got to do similar things. Like attending five John Maxwell Team Live Events. Similar environment as Paraguay. Little sleep, lots of "work", lots of studying, no time for family, but an incredible amount of energy.

Balance is a cop-out for what we truly want: a place where we belong by openly being ourselves without filters.

Balance is the make-belief that to be fulfilled all areas of life must progress equally and have the same quality.

I prefer the analogy of the seasons. There's a time to prep, a time to sow, a time to nurture, and a time to reap the harvest.

Life has a rhythm, it's only natural that the details of our lives will move in a rhythm also.

If there's one thing to take away from this idea is to recognize the freeing feeling of focusing energy on aligning the areas of life relative to a specific objective rather than ensuring they are all treated equally.

See you in the next chapter where *I share a few tactics to purposely claim your space.*

As always, this is a journey. Allow yourself to explore and discover. There's no right or wrong answer. Take what you need, test it, and adapt as you learn new things about yourself.

Chapter 12: The Simplest Way to Start Claiming Your Space

Maybe your life is not falling apart; maybe it's falling together. Don't fearfully hold on to what needs to end. The familiar life crumbles so the new life can begin.

~Bryant McGill

The previous three chapters covered three mental barriers that can sabotage any progress in living in alignment with who we are. As a quick reminder, the three barriers are: ***other people's agendas, the need to get it right, and the desire for balance.***

The following four chapters discuss four core practices of ***Purposely Claiming Your Space.***

It is logical to think that if I want to create a new life, the simplest first step is to make room for the new. Once I remove distractions and what doesn't serve me anymore, the new things can enter my life. But since I don't want everything to come in, certain rules must be in place to validate what can enter.

Furthermore, a mission or goal can be used to align efforts towards making my vision a reality. Since the vision is something I haven't done before, help will be needed along the way. But it must be people who believe in what I am trying to accomplish and want to join the journey.

Finally, life is always changing so continuous improvement and adjustments are needed.

In an attempt to simplify my reasoning, I summarized it into four practices:

1. Filter The Noise: The Art of Pruning
2. A Fenced Playground is Better: Boundaries Create Freedom
3. Never Do It Alone But Not Everyone Should Be Invited
4. Reinvent Continuously: Success Demands Growth

Remember, this is your journey so take what resonates, test it, and adapt it to what's in alignment with your discoveries from steps one and two of the framework.

Practice #1 - Filter The Noise: The Art of Pruning

I, like many others, used to think that the first step to personal improvement was to find another proven strategy to add to my already crowded to-do list so I could better manage time, live with purpose, and have a work-life balance.

I missed the idea that the easiest way to clean things up is to throw them away rather than neatly organize them.

For whatever reason, it seems like the first thing we try to do is to make everything fit by maximizing our space available. That's why we have closets hoarding items that we haven't used in years.

How much energy does it drain to figure out how to fit in one more thing in a crowded schedule?

The first practice to claiming your space is to master the art of pruning.

This is a concept I heard from Dr. Henry Cloud in his book *"Necessary Endings."*

It comes from the analogy of growing a great rose bush. Dr. Henry observed that master gardeners invested a lot of energy pruning the rose bush. And there were three options for pruning.

Option #1 - Prune What's Already Dead

This is the easiest option because it is all about removing people, activities, things, places, etc. that stop helping you in any form.

These are likened to the things in our closest that we haven't used in a year and don't even plan on using soon.

They occupy mental, emotional, or physical space and add zero value to anything we are looking to do.

- The friend, colleague, or neighbor we keep saying we will build a better relationship with but never get to it.
- The program, book, or resource we never used but feel pressured to keep because we paid for it.
- The places we seem obligated to go to.
- The people we "have" to see because of certain responsibilities but that don't get us closer to our goal.

It's easy to think that one is becoming selfish by removing these people, places, and items from our lives but the fact is that something that occupies space in our lives and doesn't help us get to where we want to go, is something that doesn't serve us and is not valuable to creating a life worthy of us.

Is it possible to turn things around with certain people or find a way to use the items and places?

Absolutely, but how likely is it that we will invest the time to figure it out when we are already committed to other things?

Wouldn't it be better to make room for something that we know will add value right away?

Option #2 - Prune What's Draining Energy And Won't Change

A rose bush can have sick branches that won't be able to recover. These branches take energy away from the healthy branches and buds.

When I started pruning my life, there were certain people, places, and things that actively drained my energy.

I would get stressed, angry, and frustrated just by thinking about it. Like a thorn stuck between my nail and finger and I couldn't reach.

I identified that I was keeping those things in my life because I felt obligated or fear missing something.

- I had to attend certain work events because my title required it even though I had no reason to be there.
- I had to interact with person X because they had status and could improve my career (like a boss).
- I listened to the news because I thought I needed to keep up to date on what's going on in the world.

- I kept interacting with certain friends because we had spent several years together.

These are people, places, and items that intentionally or not take energy from us and add unnecessary weight on our shoulders.

I believe it's easy to identify the things and places that are a negative influence in our lives.

- If every time you read the news you end up angry, frustrated, or worried, that's a good candidate to prune.
- If every time you meet with a friend, all they do is complain and criticize, that's a good candidate to prune.
- If certain social gatherings do nothing more than pass time, that's a good candidate to prune.
- If an item you use is more of a hassle than the benefit it gives, that's a good candidate to prune.

These are easy to identify, the challenge comes from the emotional and psychological attachment to them.

It's difficult to cut off interaction with a friend, coworker, or neighbor because one may think that's being impolite. However, I think we all naturally know that it's much better for both parties when each side leaves the conversation with positive energy.

With things and places, the emotional attachment to them becomes an anchor that prevents us from letting go. It's the money, time, and effort spent on it. The economists call it *sunk cost.*

The more we invest in something, the more we value it even though we know full well that it isn't helping us reach our goal.

These challenges can be overcome by shifting the measuring stick.

- Does X consistently give me energy or drain it?
- If I continue to use this item or place, will it consistently get me closer to who I want to be and what I want to accomplish?
- Does Y truly excite me?
- Do I feel obligated to engage with Z or fear that if I don't engage with it something bad will happen?

These are questions I used to rate people, items, and places relative to my discoveries from Step #2 of the framework, courageously discover your light.

Option #3 - Prune The Good Stuff to Make Room For The Great

This is the hardest of them all, which is why I mentioned it in third place.

It's the most challenging because we are raised to believe in *"if it's not broken, why fix it?"*

I consider this the option to be used once we have completed the other two.

Some say that a rose bush produces more buds than it can handle. And it seems like life does the same thing.

There's always a new project or idea to pursue, there's a new relationship that can be developed, a new program, or another task to do. Life seems filled with opportunities to do something but the human body has a limited capacity.

Thus, there comes a time where an aspiring entrepreneur must quit a high-paying job to focus their energy on scaling their business. Or, an athlete has to let go of one sport so they can be a highly paid professional athlete on another.

The choices won't always be as extreme as the examples above but they are challenging.

I have had to stop seeing good friends when the relationship became one-sided.

Or, I have had to trade time for certain activities to focus on a business opportunity.

The key to deciding on this area rides on the clarity of your vision, values, and purpose.

There's only so much time, mental capacity, and hours in a day to make the vision a reality and sometimes something good must be paused or stopped indefinitely to focus all energy and resources on the one thing that will get the ball rolling forward faster and stronger.

It's about increasing the intensity of our efforts towards achieving a certain outcome.

A Suggested Pruning Process

1. Have your purpose, values, vision, goals, and strengths in front of you.
2. List all the people, things, activities, places, projects, and commitments you have.
3. Take each item on the list and rate it against your responses from #1. Here are some sample reflection questions:

    a. Does this help me express my purpose?

    b. Does it help me develop myself and aid the pursuit of my vision and goals?

    c. Is it in alignment with what I am trying to accomplish going forward?

    d. How much would I miss it if I stopped doing it?

    e. How much would I miss them if I stopped interacting with this person?

    f. How much better would my life be if this wasn't present in my life?

    g. How would I feel if I didn't do X?

4. You get the point, it's all about alignment and keeping the things that help us be better and/or move forward. Everything else is up for removal.

One last thing, when dealing with people, some circumstances will prevent you from completely removing a person from your life. That's when boundaries come into play, which is what I discuss in the next practice.

Chapter 13: The Counterintuitive Benefit of Boundaries

I find it fascinating how the human spirit wants to be free but there's a need for boundaries or game rules.

Simon Sinek talks about the circle of safety. In the early days of civilization, the circle of safety was the territory dominated by the tribe one belongs to. It allowed a person to operate freely and without harm.

Marking territory was a way to keep the harmful things away so the tribe could thrive.

Similarly, boundaries seem necessary for the mind to function properly.

I cannot recall where I read the following analogy but it made sense and sets the stage for the second practice of purposely claiming your space.

Suppose life is represented as a playground.

The playground doesn't have a fence initially and it's surrounded by busy streets.

As the children go out to play, one has to be constantly watching out for the adventurous children who want to go beyond the playground. It's dangerous to get on the street.

Every break, one has to constantly be aware of the children's movements.

Now, supposed a fenced is installed around the playground making it safer for the children to move freely within the confines of the playground.

One no longer has to worry about children accidentally getting hit by a car or getting lost.

The children's movements may be limited to the area of the playground but they now don't have to worry about us scolding them about staying inside the playground, or that they can get lost, or hit by a car.

There's no danger. They now can be as creative as they want within the confines of the playground.

There's a sense of freedom even though the space is limited.

Practice #2 - A Fenced Playground Is Better: Boundaries Create Freedom

Let's see if I can relate this to setting boundaries for us to have greater freedom to create a life worthy of us.

Whenever we think of rules and boundaries, we tend to focus on the things we are losing. But the value of boundaries comes from what we have to gain.

I should clarify that boundaries aren't meant to be thought of as permanent since the playground can always be expanded.

Back to the analogy...

By having no boundaries for our lives, we are letting everything freely come in and out of our lives.

It's like the closet that no matter how much time one spends taking things out, something else quickly comes in and takes its place.

Whatever was pruned will be quickly replaced by something else that doesn't serve our cause.

Another thing that happens when there aren't any boundaries is that we are constantly on the lookout for new things and activities. Life is so open we don't know what to focus on and what's important. With free-range, one could go anywhere!

By setting boundaries, we can reduce our line of sight temporarily and keep out the distractions and dangers. We can have a space where we can focus on what needs to get done. Without distractions and the fear of getting lost, we can give way for our creativity to come forth. We can choose what to do and when to do so. Life becomes the place where we be, do, and have whatever we want.

Boundaries are the strategies we can implement to protect our time, resources, and energy from negative influences and distractions so we can make room for creativity and focus on what will help us create the life we want.

Here are three ways to create boundaries: protect your time, have a definite goal, and have a way to prioritize.

Protect Your Time

> *"Your time is limited, so don't waste it living someone else's life."*
>
> *~Steve Jobs*

I have to admit a love-hate relationship with schedules and time management systems. I like the idea of flexibility and having to fill my calendar with specific slots dedicated to specific tasks feels constricting.

But there's something powerful about blocking time for specific things. It doesn't have to be a full-scale project management approach but it is helpful to focus the mind on a specific objective for a period of time.

For claiming your space, protecting time is about making room for you to focus on creating the things you want and not what's on other people's agenda. It's not about being selfish but about ensuring you have the freedom to do this on your time, your schedule, and your priorities.

As the wise book says in Ecclesiastes chapter three verse one, *"There is a season for everything, a time for every occupation under heaven."*

- **A time for yourself:** this is the time for reflection and self-study. To find what's working and what isn't. To take care of yourself.
- **A time for relationships:** this is for nurturing relationships in whatever activity you desire. It's an intentional time to grow in life with others.

- **A time for work:** it's self-explanatory but it helps to explicitly tell yourself when you plan to work.
- **A time for entertainment:** this is for relaxing and enjoying life.
- **A time to grow:** this is a specific time for reinventing yourself and hone your skills through whichever you desire: books, programs, seminars, experiments, etc.
- **A time to rest:** besides sleep, it's also helpful to have a period to simply do nothing and allow the body, mind, and soul to rest.

I'm sure you can come up with many other categorizations but these are the ones I have used depending on the seasons of life.

The point of this is not to fit every category into every single day but for you to determine how you want to allocate your time throughout the week for the activities to help you build your vision.

Sometimes, certain areas will need more time than others but what matters is that one intentionally chooses how to use time and have guidelines on who and what gets to be a part of it.

Here are a few ideas to try as you work to figure out your style:

- Set specific days and times of the week where people can schedule lunch with you.
- Determine a specific day of the week, or time of day, where people can ask you to be in meetings.
- Block a specific time of the day for focused work. A period of time solely for working on complex projects without distractions.

- Come up with a set of questions to determine whether you are needed in a meeting or it's something you can address with a quick chat.
- Have a specific time to check email and don't check it outside of that time.
- Have office hours for walk-in help and support. Avoid helping walk-ins right away if you know it will take longer than two minutes to do so.

Come up with a quick rating system to decide whether you should go to an event or not.

Have a do not disturb exception list. A list of 3-5 people or things you allow yourself to attend immediately no matter what you are doing.

There are many other examples and objections one can come up with for setting time boundaries but what matters is that we have a set of guidelines to help us quickly decide whether something or someone is worthy of our time.

The key here is to be intentional with time, not just have an open door to come in and out whenever they want to.

It's your playground, not theirs. Your house, your rules.

Have A Definite Goal Not a S.M.A.R.T. One

With time management strategies, goal setting is a common practice.

The SMART goals system is one of the most used but that's not what I am talking about here for a few reasons.

First, I am not a fan of the application.

The letters stand for specific, measurable, attainable, realistic, and time-bound. And, I only agree with two, maybe three.

Specific

It does make sense to have a specific goal because it brings clarity to what we are building and it also helps the mind avoid confusion.

Measurable

They say that what gets measured can be improved and gets done. My point of contention with it is that not everything that can be measured counts, and not everything that counts can be measured.

Attainable & Realistic

For making our vision a reality, it will be very challenging to determine what's realistic or attainable because we are trying to do something we have never done before.

Even if we allow someone else to help us determine how attainable and realistic is our dream, they aren't qualified to do so because they don't know our full potential.

Most people use their past to determine how attainable is a goal but the past cannot determine a future that's going to be different.

Time-Bound

This one makes sense to me, not as a definition of success and failure but to simply give the mind a deadline. A deadline creates focus. This is the reason some people are super effective at work the few days before they go on a long vacation.

The time limit helps us focus our energy and measure progress relative to passing time. It also creates a sense of urgency.

Now, I don't believe there's success or failure based on whether the goal is achieved before or after the deadline. This journey is about progress and focusing our energy on creating something better than we have had before.

A time deadline is also helpful to give an allotted amount of time to figure something out and avoid getting lost in a rabbit hole.

The latter helps when trying to decide. Rather than wasting countless hours researching and analyzing data, we can set a deadline to simply decide after a certain time has passed based on whatever information is available at the moment. Acting is more valuable than trying to get it right because it produces feedback. And with feedback, adjustments can be made.

Recall, it's easier to steer a car when it's moving.

The Type of Goal I Am Talking About
What I am talking about is the goal that explains the existence of the fenced playground. It's the type of play, the number of objects inside of it, the proper use of equipment, and who's allowed to use it.

I know this could sound a little restrictive but the intent is to have a designated purpose.

The goal is clear, definite, lacks ambiguity, and has a set time for its accomplishment.

The challenge comes in what clear and definite means.

Goal clarity is about having a description of the objective in such a way that one has no confusion about what success looks like.

Most people set goals like losing weight or make X amount of money. Yes, those apply but those aren't the only categories for creating a life worthy of us.

A clear goal could be as simple as committing to meet one friend a week for at least one hour to catch up and enjoy the time. Or, it can be something like stipulating a set time of day to pray, meditate, or journal.

Clarity has a level of specificity that allows us to visualize it happening.

Regarding a definite goal, I see it from the perspective of commitment. The goal is so void of confusion I can easily commit to its accomplishment. It's an extension of clarity.

Now, many commit the mistake of confusing the word *"definite"* with *"extensive and thorough"*. The latter is just an excuse to prepare and must be avoided at all costs.

A definite goal doesn't need a 100-page execution plan that addresses all the possible scenarios.

A definite goal is like saying I will eat a cheeseburger from my local favorite restaurant this Friday with a close friend.

How you get to the restaurant, which friend, and what time aren't as important as having it very clear that I want to meet with a friend for lunch on Friday to eat a cheeseburger at my favorite restaurant nearby.

This directive helps the brain filter distractions and focuses energy on achieving that goal by the designated date.

A goal is intended to help us become who we need to be to have the life we desire. It's about progress not winning or losing.

Where Should The Goal Come From?

This is where your vision comes into play. If a vision doesn't exist, maybe the first goal to have is to dedicate specific time to developing one.

A vision describes the ideal version of our future. A goal helps us get there.

1. Choose an area of life
2. Review your vision for #1
3. Determine where you are concerning the vision
4. Pick an objective that will help you get closer to making the vision a reality.
5. Get clear about what success looks like for that objective, give yourself a deadline, and commit to follow-through with it.

The goal can be developing a skill, acquiring knowledge, an activity, developing a relationship, rest, etc.

It doesn't matter what you pick, what matters is that you have a clear direction for your efforts.

One final tip about goal setting.

I have found that for me and my clients, it is easier to consistently act towards achieving a goal if we define it as the smallest possible step that can be taken to make progress.

For example, let us say I set a goal to read 52 books in a year.

• Many would set a goal and say they will read one book a week and then go nuts with it.

- To follow my rules of goal setting, I will read 52 self-development books in a year to work on self-leadership and mindset.
- Self-development books average about 250 pages, which means that's about 36 pages a day.
- Let's say it takes me two minutes to read a page. That's about 72 minutes or a little over one hour a day to read.

Most people rarely find themselves in a position to take one hour a day to read. So, while the goal is an excellent idea, the chances of a person following through with it, are low.

Hence, I propose the concept of making the goal even smaller.

Since this is about progress and enjoying the journey, why not set the goal to read at least 1-page of a book a day or 10-minutes a day.

One could think one page a day won't even get me close to one book a week. That's correct. The purpose of the goal is not to accomplish something but to become someone better.

It's easier to commit to at least one page a day of reading. What people miss is the compounding effect of consistency.

The more I can meet the 10-minute or 1-page a day goal, the more excited I would get about meeting the goal. As the days go by, the excitement turns into a "what if I can do more?"

The more I read, the faster I get at reading, and the better I get at retaining information. This will continue until I read a book a week or more, while still keeping the goal of reading at least one page or 10 minutes a day.

When I started my leadership development journey, I realized I had little time to read, but I did have a daily commute I could use to listen to a book or training program.

In a matter of six months, I had gone through at least 73 books by listening 20 minutes at a time.

Do I remember everything I listened to? No. But my mindset and behaviors changed just by listening through the concepts repeatedly.

I was also not trying to memorize everything. I was listening intending to learn about specific skills and practices.

There were books I listened to multiple times to study them. I then took notes of what I heard and developed my thoughts.

The goal was to listen to an educational resource while driving. Nothing more, nothing less.

How many people can say they have gone through 73 books in their life, let alone six months.

So, as you set your goals, pick the direction you want to go, and try setting a micro-step goal that keeps you motivated to achieve every day, and experience the power of the compounding effect of consistency.

Have A Way to Prioritize Activities

Freed from the daily struggle just to exist, we can let our time be filled with meaningless activity and motion or choose to spend it doing the things that matter most to us."

~Hyrum W. Smith

This one is also much discussed so I'll keep it brief and share the method I have found most useful.

Whether we want to agree with it or not, every human has a rating system and what matters to me may not necessarily matter to you. Hence, having a prioritization system ensures that you and I can keep what matters to us front and center.

I like this system because it incorporates personal values and preferences not just the characteristics of a project or activity.

This is the system shared by John C. Maxwell. He calls it the Three Rs: *required, rewarding, return.*

- What's required of you?
    - Whether it is life or job, this is about what is required for you to do in the specific area.
    - These are the things only you can do and no one else.
    - For example, I can have someone find my coaching clients but I need to do the coaching.
- How rewarding is it to you?
    - This about how energized you are when doing the task and how aligned it is with your values, purpose, and passion.
    - It can also be thought of as how fulfilling it would be to do the task
- What level of return does it give?
    - This is about the benefit received from doing the task.
    - It pertains to how much closer to the goal it takes you when done.

The process:

1. List all the things you are expected to do or want to do
2. Rate each item for each R-category from 1 to 10. No need to be scientific, just guesstimate it.
3. Sort each item by the total score and focus on the top 20%.

This is mostly used for to-do lists but it can be adapted to more intangible things like deciding if you should accept a lunch invitation from someone you don't know well and your schedule is already packed.

Like any other practice shared in this book, take it for a test and adjust it as needed.

The purpose of such a system is to have a structured way to make quick decisions about what you do and what gets delegated, declined, or ignored.

The three Rs can help you know how your resources are allocated and if any adjustments are needed.

You now have three ways to create boundaries. Protecting your time, having a definite goal, and the 3-Rs prioritization methods are simple but provide a strong foundation for properly focusing our efforts in creating a life worthy of us.

In the next chapter, I explore the concept of selecting who is worthy of joining your adventure

Chapter 14: Not Everyone Deserves To Hear Your Dream

"The number one reason for lack of growth in people's lives is the absence of joining forces outside themselves who push them to grow.

Instead, they keep telling themselves that they will somehow, by willpower or commitment, make themselves grow. That never works."

~Dr. Henry Cloud

It took me a while to figure this one out because I like to do things independently. I delay asking for help until the last moment and have tried many ways to get it done.

At the beginning of the journey, I was in a position where I wasn't sure who to trust with my decision.

Furthermore, I had an internal struggle between having a certain level of ego where I didn't want to admit needing help and the excitement of wanting to tell everybody what I was up to hoping they could help.

Unfortunately, when I shared that I wanted to switch over to focusing on leadership development and life coaching, most people in my life remembered me as...

- ...the actuary
- ...the know-it-all
- ...the person that thinks it's my way or the highway.

They knew me as anything else except who I wanted to become. Thus, they were quick to push back.

- How are you going to do that?
- What makes you think you can do it?
- Who's going to help you?
- Why don't you just finish your actuarial exams and make more money?
- Why don't you just keep doing the things you've been doing because it seems to work?
- You say you want to be a speaker and trainer? Better work on your delivery and emotional intelligence first.

They were giving me all this feedback to help me stay safe but not necessarily support me.

Today, I think of these individuals as giving all that advice to make sure I still fit their model of the world and the mental box they put me in.

In contrast, during my leadership development journey, as I facilitated a symposium and participated in several personal development opportunities, I connected with people who had similar values and objectives, including some who were ready to listen to what I had to say and where I was going.

These differing experiences reminded me that *we must be careful with who a dream is shared because their words and actions have the power to fuel or drain our conviction.*

The latter is the essence of *practice #3 of claiming your space: never do it alone but not everyone should be invited.*

We have enough doubt and things to worry about when endeavoring into the unknown to be dealing with someone else's lack of imagination and support for our dreams.

I share more about who is worth listening to in *Step #4 of the framework, confidently filter your critics.*

This practice is about being humble enough to recognize our strengths and abilities aren't enough to create our ideal future.

So, the question now is *"who is worthy of hearing the dream?"*

Deciding Who to Invite on The Journey

This doesn't mean the person has to be like a business partner and always be involved in the process but it has to be someone willing to help you brainstorm solutions, make it safe for you to share your struggles and work through them, or assist you with some of the work.

These people can serve any support role in your journey. The key is that they are invested in helping you achieve your vision.

There are many ways to identify these people but what I have found to work best for me is to pay attention to the person's reaction and nonverbal communication when sharing your ideas with them.

Most people will help you by giving you feedback intended to help you stay safe in your comfort zone. The same people would quickly jump into giving you a solution to your problems before they understand what you're trying to accomplish.

Most of these advisers have never done what you're trying to do and are simply relaying what they have heard from others or imposing their limiting beliefs on you.

So, why should you listen to them? You shouldn't. I'll expand on this in *Step #4 - Confidently Filter Your Critics.*

Unfortunately, often, family, friends, and loved ones are part of this group of people who zap the energy out of our dreams under the pretense they are trying to help us stay safe and avoid mistakes.

It can be painful to not invite them on your journey but this is about you creating a life worthy of you; and that means keeping sharing dreams to a minimum to satiate their curiosity and move the conversation along.

Who should be invited? The individuals that when sharing your dream with them,

- You notice the excitement in their eyes,
- You sense their energy rise,
- They focus on what you're saying,
- They pose questions about your purpose and where you're trying to go,
- They give you ideas to make it better rather than try to push back and pull you back to *"reality,"*
- They give you more ideas and add fuel to the fire, and,
- At some point, they may even ask to be part of it.

These individuals genuinely say,

- I would like to help you
- How can I help you?
- How can I be a part of this?
- Is it money, is it resources, is it a thinking partnership?
- Should I connect you with someone?

You notice they volunteer to help you.

The key is paying attention to the energy before, during, and after the conversation.

If after sharing your dream, you leave that conversation excited and with greater energy, the person you talked to is worth considering inviting on the journey.

If you find yourself in a conversation where the person is quick to tell you why it will not work, dismiss the idea, or drains your energy, you know that is someone not worth sharing your dreams with anymore.

Why Is This Selection Process Valuable?

"The time to nurse an idea is at the time of its birth. Every minute it lives, gives it a better chance of surviving.

The FEAR OF CRITICISM is at the bottom of the destruction of most ideas which never reach the PLANNING and ACTION stage."

~Napoleon Hill

A dream has to be nurtured. Its fire must be tended to.

When we share dreams with people that are not willing to tend to the fire, we risk the chance of letting our dream die because someone else convinces us we shouldn't be doing it.

Initially, we're doing something we haven't done before. We're going to have doubts, we're going to fear things not working. And, we don't need more people adding to that stress.

What we need is people that can encourage us to keep going despite fear and doubt. People that can help us get clear on what we want, where we're going, identify the tools we have at our disposal, and lend a hand to help us create what we want.

I end this practice with a clarification: **this is not about finding yes people.**

This is not about finding people quick to say yes to everything I say. This is about finding individuals who make us better.

Sometimes they'll push back to help us gain clarity and explore alternative solutions. But the important part of it all is that they keep the mindset to help us succeed instead of keeping us *"safe."*

There's a difference in energy between the two groups. Unfortunately, I don't have a good way to explain it, it has to be something experienced as you engage with others.

Hence, pay attention, put it to the test, and identify your way to decide who you share your dreams with.

Chapter 15: The Dream Demands Reinvention

*"We cannot become what we need to be
by remaining what we are."*

~Max DePree

In step #2 of the framework, you worked on describing the ideal version of your life. Most likely, this vision includes many things you have never done before and have no clue where to begin.

Additionally, advances in technology and access to new information continuously changes the way the world operates. The practices of today can be obsolete tomorrow. And, whatever worked before may stop working at any time.

It's a hassle and it's also the way of the universe.

The only constant in life is change. The only way to keep up with it is to continue evolving.

We know what we want, why we want it, what tools we can use to get it, and what is non-negotiable. But we don't know how to put it all together.

Combine the lack of how-to knowledge with the constant changes of life and we can easily lose hope if we stay attached to wanting to be right, worrying about other people's opinions, and maintaining balance.

Gladly, there is the alternative I have been reinforcing throughout the book, *"give yourself permission to explore and discover."*

This journey is about constantly finding ways to learn more about ourselves, what we can do, and how we engage with the world so we can discover ways to realize our vision.

The constant change of life demands adaptation.

Often, we focus on "how can this get done?" when we should be focusing on "who must I become to be, do, and have what I claim to want?"

The former question focuses on tasks and what needs to happen to achieve a certain goal.

The latter focuses on the individual. It encompasses mind, body, and soul. It's not just about skills but all facets of life.

We can use the lottery to illustrate this idea.

The first question would focus on finding a way to win the lottery; the second, seeks to identify who the person needs to be to manage what happens after they win.

There's a reason why most lottery winners are broke soon after they win millions. They simply weren't ready to manage the responsibility of that level of money.

Similarly, realizing our vision will require a different version of us. It requires different beliefs, habits, skills, relationships, finances, etc.

As the best-selling book by Marshall Goldsmith states, *"What Got You Here Won't Get You There."*

This is the fourth practice of claiming your space, *"REINVENT YOURSELF CONTINUOUSLY: SUCCESS DEMANDS GROWTH."*

How to Grow

Before sharing a generic process, I summarize its intent with John Maxwell's Law of the Rubber Band, ***"Growth Stops When You Lose The Tension Between Where You Are and Where You Could Be."***

It provides a great visual for what growth means to me.

A rubber band is only useful when it is stretched. The greater the stretch the stronger the grip. Granted, too much of a stretch and the rubber band breaks.

Hence, the key to growth is to seek to *"stretch"* beyond our emotional, mental, and physical capabilities to prepare for the challenges ahead.

Another analogy I like to use is muscle growth.

The only way to increase our muscular mass is to force the muscle to work harder than before. This can be done by handling greater weight than normal or increasing time under tension.

What many don't realize is that when a muscle is working harder than normal, its fibers stretch. Some fibers break and others don't revert back to their original form.

It is the restoration of the broken and overextended fibers that causes muscle growth.

If exercise is taken too far, injury can happen.

The same applies to personal development. The only way we can become who we need to be to handle our dream is to purposely find ways to be outside our normal circumstances.

The method or medium doesn't matter. The objective is to identify the gaps between the future and current version of you so you can determine possible actions steps.

As with other exercises in this book, focus on one area at a time. Here is the general plan of attack.

This process is similar to the one proposed in the goal-setting practice.

1. Look at the vision outline
2. Determine the gaps (skills, mindset, habits, relationships, knowledge, etc.)
3. Pick one gap to focus on for a specific set of time.
4. Find people, programs, or resources to help you improve in the chosen area.
5. Rinse and repeat.

If I were to suggest a place to start, I'd share the one I used. I followed John Maxwell's book, "The 15 Invaluable Laws of Growth."

1. Read one chapter at a time.

2. Collect insights, thoughts, and questions from the reading.
3. Answer the exercise questions at the end of each chapter.
4. Identify something to work on for the week or month.
5. Evaluate progress at the end of the week or month.
6. Keep what worked and discard the rest.
7. Repeat steps 1-6 with each chapter.

Some chapters may connect better than others, but the practice of purposely testing the concepts in each chapter gradually changed the way I approached life and increased my self-awareness.

Whether you try using John's book or something else, the key is to focus on one thing at a time, monitor results, and keep what works.

Talk to you in the next chapter where I discuss how to deal with the biggest barrier I have experienced when creating a life worthy of me.

Chapter 16: Feedback is Unavoidable, Listening is Optional

"No battle plan survives first contact with the enemy."

~Helmuth von Moltke the Elder

By now, the journey to stop seeking validation and thriving your way has begun. Others may have noticed the changes; some, may even comment on them.

Also, you may have seen that no matter how detailed and thorough the plan, when it is all set and done, the steps taken to achieve success are always different from the original plan.

As soon as the first action is taken, something goes wrong and adjustments must be made to proceed.

Thankfully, the Internet has a plethora of content discussing the many tactics and strategies one can use to overcome the sticking points.

Step #4 of the Greatness Within Framework is not about the external game but about dealing with *self-judgment* and *criticism from others*. Things I consider the top killers of dreams.

The strategies and tactics to overcome an obstacle are easy to find and apply. What paralyzes the person and kills the dream is criticism.

Step #4 of the framework focuses on helping you *confidently filter your critics.*

The way I see it, there are only two groups of critics: *myself and others.*

I address the most powerful of the two first, self-judgment.

Judgment Day: How To Say Goodbye To Your Old Self

> *"One cannot be prepared for something while secretly believing it will not happen."*
>
> ~Nelson Mandela

Just as I said we are the only ones who can know how far we can go and what we want, we are also the only ones who can keep score on everything we do.

We spend every second of the day with ourselves and our brains can unconsciously record everything we experience and do.

Since the brain keeps a record of all our successes and failures, not surprisingly, it is the first and most influential critic on our journey.

- Who do you think you are?
- Who will listen to you?
- Are you crazy? You have never done this before!
- Are you going to throw your education away?

- It's too late to do something new.
- That makes no money. How are you going to feed your family?
- No one listens to you now, what makes you think someone will?

These are a few sentences I said to myself when I shifted my focus towards leadership development and mindset coaching.

Let me address the three most common self-criticisms I hear.

Self-Judgment #1 - Who Do You Think You Are?

I strongly believe this is not a self-made criticism. I believe this is our internalization of other people's voices.

For as long as I can remember, we are raised to think we have to earn everything we want. Society makes us think that we aren't mature enough to do what we want.

- That's for grown-ups
- You need to go to college first
- You need money for that
- You don't know yourself enough, yet
- You are still a kid
- Stop daydreaming

Sometimes the voices are subtle and innocent, and other times, they are brunt.

Slowly the mind develops the idea that we aren't ready and that we have a long list of to-dos before we can make a difference in our lives and others.

"Who do you think you are" presents itself as a safety mechanism by the ego to say "be careful, you ain't ready for that, yet! Let's get back to what we were doing before and remember our place."

I heard this from so many people trying to *"keep me safe"* throughout my life that at some point I believed it and simply did it myself.

Self-Judgment #2 - You Have Never Done It Before What Makes You Think You Can?

Got to love this one because it's a logical argument based on evidence.

The brain seems to have a natural bias to be a historian and a reporter.

The **historian brain** enjoys looking at our recorded past, which is everything we have ever experienced, and uses it to make sense of the present and predict the future.

The **reporter brain** is a master at analyzing circumstances and adds them to our history to determine whether an idea will work or not.

These characteristics are so ingrained in human behavior we use them everywhere.

- We use a resume to determine whether a person will be able to do a specific job.
- We use our past to determine whether a goal is realistic.
- We look at our bank account to determine whether we can buy something or not.
- We decide whether we will like someone by comparing them to our past relationships.

While the past and present can inform the future, they are not causative of it. The future is created by the actions taken in the present moment.

Self-Judgment #3 - There's No Money in That, Don't Bother

How often do you hear something like "don't be a musician, you will starve to death"?

It's interesting how often we use money as the decision-maker.

A mentor called it the "Money May I" mindset.

The problem with the "money may I" mindset is that the first response is always "no."

There are infinite examples of it and the flow can be summarized like this...

1. I'd love to travel to country X and stay there for a month.
2. Your historian brain goes to the memory bank and checks if there's enough money to do it.
3. Then it responds, "Sorry there's not enough money for it and we have bills coming up", or "Sorry, that's not in the budget", or "Nope, that's too expensive."
4. End of discussion

We are so used to the "money may I" process that we don't even try to figure out how much is it going to cost, how quickly can we save the money, or brainstorm ways we could make some extra money.

The process was simply "Money can I.....don't even bother asking...the answer is no."

Other people would do the same to us whenever we share an idea with them. We haven't finished sharing our idea and they are already saying...

- ...where are you going to get the money for that?
- ...do you have enough money for that?
- ...does that make any money?
- ...how are you going to afford it?

It's like *money* becomes the ruler of the universe.

Take Your Gremlins to Court

Since our inner critic likes to pretend to be logical, the best approach I have used against it is what one of my previous mentors, Ed DeCosta called, *"take your gremlins to court."*

The process is self-explanatory.

Each self-criticism is considered a gremlin in our head trying to wreak havoc and dissuade us from pursuing something greater than us.

Therefore, we take each gremlin to court and force it to prove to us beyond a reasonable doubt they are stating the truth.

The exercise is straightforward:

1. List all the reasons you think you won't be able to change your situation.
2. List the evidence you have to prove it.
3. Find evidence to disprove your case.

The objective is to realize self-criticisms are not absolute and are based on one or two instances we then extrapolate to other events and carry for the rest of our lives.

Let's look at the previous criticisms.

Who do you think you are? You aren't ready for it. Regardless of the proof, we are an individual on a mission to create a different life. If we aren't mistaken, the current life is created by our past actions; thus, the new life requires learning new things and becoming a different person. We may not be ready to have that life right now but we can evolve just as prior generations have done it.

You have never done it before so what makes you think you can? Yes, we haven't done it in our past but the same thing happened when I learned to swim, drive a car, use the computer, finish school, etc. All those things at the time were things I had not done before, yet, I can do it, now. Therefore, I can probably learn what I need to make this vision a reality.

That makes no money. Well, I notice that at least one person is doing well in what I am seeking to do. So, why can't I do something similar? If someone can make a living playing a video game, I'm sure there's a way to make a living with what I am trying to do.

As you can see from the hypothetical answers, *"taking your gremlins to court"* is all about finding examples that disprove the criticism. It's more powerful to have personal examples but it's okay to use other people as examples.

It's possible that when using other people's success as examples, the ego would say *"but you aren't them"* which is just another version of the "who do you think you are" argument. Yes, the ego is correct but that doesn't erase the fact that someone else is doing it.

Thank You For Your Service

When I first heard the concept I'm sharing shortly, I struggled to accept it.

It's difficult to see how the inner critic is serving us. The inner critic is a tool our ego uses to keep us safe. It's a survival mechanism that forms its criteria based on what it knows about ourselves and the world.

Here's an example.

> When I was five years old, I was running around with my cousin. We were role-playing some war scene. As we ran to the backyard, his dogs, a German Shepherd, and a small dog were playing around.
>
> At some point, I ended in a corner behind the two dogs.
>
> The dogs were biting each other when I scared the German Shepherd with a loud noise.
>
> The dog quickly jumped back and grabbed my head with his jaws.
>
> I don't remember how long I was caught inside the dog's mouth. I don't remember being in pain.
>
> I just remember the fear and crying.

The rest of the story isn't necessary to assume that any child that goes through such experience would develop an aversion to dogs.

Many who hear the story are quick to ask me if I fear dogs.

Yet, I don't.

I interpreted the event differently. I see it as my fault I got bitten. I interrupted the dog's activity with my loud noise and paid for it.

The dog didn't mean harm, he was defending himself.

I was in the wrong.

Now, where would I get that idea from?

I don't know where it comes from but I speculate is related to how I observed my father deal with life.

What matters is that the same mindset shows up throughout my life.

I have entered work relationships where people have taken advantage of me and I still take full responsibility for it.

The ego shows up saying, *"remember this is going to be your fault if it goes wrong, so make sure to be thorough and thoughtful before you do it. You don't want to get hurt like that time the German Shepherd almost ate you alive."*

Hence, I seek to be perfect and have everything figured out before I launch into something new.

This is just one of the many pieces of evidence my ego would use to substantiate the need for overthinking.

Today, I recognize the inner critic as a mechanism of safety created by a past version of myself who didn't have the knowledge I have now.

Many get sucked into coming up with clever ways to ignore, eliminate, or crush the inner critic, not realizing that since the ego knows everything we think, know, and do, it's always one step ahead looking out for our safety.

It takes too much effort to outwit myself. War begets war.

The solution?

What I have found works better is to simply thank the inner critic for their service.

> *Thank you for bringing this to my attention. That's a great observation and it's valid based on your perspective and the information you have at your disposal. From your vantage point, it makes total sense. Thank you!*
>
> *Fortunately, I have learned things since you learned about the world. Thank you for bringing me this far. It's time for a new way of doing things and I know it's possible.*
>
> *I acknowledge your input and you can now go on your merry way. Thank you.*

This approach works because the ego likes to be acknowledged and appreciated. It's the same response I have when I know the other person heard what I had to say and valued it regardless of whether they use it or not.

Thus, the next time the inner critic shows up you can try taking them to court, thanking them for their input, or a combination of both.

If neither of these methods work, go to your support system and ask them to help you shift perspective.

Eric Hoffer said it best, *"No matter what our achievements might be, we think well of ourselves only in rare moments. We need people to bear witness against our inner judge, who keeps a book on our shortcomings and transgressions. We need people to convince us that we are not as bad as we think we are."*

Let's move on to dealing with criticism from others.

Navigating The Land Of The Walking Dead

"Great spirits have always encountered violent opposition from mediocre minds."

~Albert Einstein

If you are engaging with the thoughts shared in this book, you have likely noticed yourself feeling different from others.

Maybe, you noticed that most people are out there trying to be like other people. Like a version of *keeping up with the Joneses* not from the rich lifestyle perspective but simply imitating some fictional ideal person.

I visualize it as most people are in line moving towards something that no one knows what it is but they all think it's great.

My break room event was my stepping out of the line and trying to figure out what the heck is going on.

In my mind, I think of it as living in the land of the walking dead.

What does that mean?

In the walking dead universe, most people are moving around like zombies. They don't have an intellect; they simply move around looking for food and wherever the days would take them.

They all seem to operate the same way. They are attracted by loud noises and identify food by the way something smells.

They have slow and predictable behavior.

I observe similar behavior in society.

The first time I mentioned to my mom I wanted to become a leadership trainer, she did what most people do. She told me all the things I needed to change and improve upon before I dared to begin.

The same thing happened the first time I shared with coworkers that I would host a Leadership Development Summit. They immediately said it would not work and pointed out that I needed money to find speakers, conference rooms, and audio/video equipment.

This happens all the time with well-meaning intentions.

But I found that most people I interact with are simply relaying information they hear from someone else rather than the wisdom that comes from their experience and application of proven principles.

I also noticed that most people are simply trying to mimic someone else because *"that's what everyone is doing"* rather than determining for themselves whether something fits or not.

They are simply falling in line repeating what everyone else is doing because that seems to be the safest bet.

"Two percent of the people think; three percent of the people think they think, and ninety-five percent of the people would rather die than think."

~George Bernard Shaw

Thus, we move through life walking among people who have it in their best interest for us to step in line because it can be troublesome if someone breaks the flow of the line.

I call this group of people the *"Walking Dead" because they are simply in our lives to make us average.* They may have ambitions but have settled for what they have and they do not seem to want others to succeed. It's the adage, "misery loves company."

It's the 98% of people who think they are helping us but are simply trying to keep us where we are.

How to Navigate The Walking Dead's Feedback?

The objective here is to use the discoveries from *Step #2 - Courageously Discover Your Light* to determine whose feedback is worth considering.

There are **three (3)** ideas or questions I recall whenever someone is giving their constructive criticism or opinion about an idea or behavior of mine.

#1 - It is my dream, not yours

I am the one who is going to feel the pain of regret or the satisfaction of pursuing what I love.

Someone can provide feedback, persuade us to stop, or share possible solutions but the decision is mine to continue or not.

They will not reach the end of my life with *"what ifs."*

I rather fail knowing I gave it my all than live a comfortable life wondering.

#2 - If they haven't lived it, they don't count?
I have been one of those people who gives a lot of knowledge, solutions, and criticism without proving the concepts I have shared.

Knowledge is easy to gather, especially now that we have the Internet at our disposal. It's easy to come up with our theoretical conclusions without any evidence behind them.

While a certain principle has been proven by others, it doesn't apply to everyone and in every situation.

If I have not been through the same experiences as the recipient of my feedback and attempted to do what they are trying to accomplish, I have no business claiming to have the answers. I can share what I have heard from others and think on the matter but it should come with a disclaimer.

Unfortunately, too many people like to relay information claiming it as true without ever doing the proper fact-checking or support it with personal experience.

If the person has done nothing similar before, their feedback doesn't matter. It's all speculation.

What happens if the person has had experience doing what we are trying to do?

That's a valid question and a common situation.

The question here is: *have they had success applying what they are sharing with you?*

If the answer is "no," then the feedback given is a candidate to be ignored or information that can be used to avoid pitfalls in our approach.

If you decide to use the person's experience of failure to learn, remember that just because something didn't work for them, doesn't mean it won't work for you.

The proper approach is to take the information, test it, and go from there. It's applying critical thinking.

#3 - Success is not enough.
Let's say the person succeeds in doing what I am trying to do and their feedback is sound. *Should I take their ideas and run with them?*

Not necessarily...

There are infinite ways of solving a problem.

It only takes a few minutes of research to see there are several success stories in any endeavor one can think of.

The same research will reveal that the mechanisms to achieve success vary from person to person and company to company.

Let's recall that claiming your space implies aligning everything we do to who we think we are.

So, what's left to check? **The person's values and character.**

This is part of the non-negotiable identified in step #2 of the framework.

Today, we have a negative image of Adolf Hitler. Yet, we miss the fact that he led a country towards becoming a massive threat to the world. That's no small achievement.

It can be said Hitler was a leader but what made him a negative influence was his set of values.

It is an extreme example but it helps illustrate the importance of evaluating a person's feedback based on their character and values.

If someone achieved their success by cutting corners and manipulating information, is that who we want to model?

> *"I care not what others think of what I do, but I care very much about what I think of what I do! That is character!"*
>
> *~Theodore Roosevelt*

Waking Up The Dead

I shared earlier in the book that I found an audience when I led the weekly Leadership Symposium.

It's interesting the way it happened because I didn't want to do it initially.

This was a group I was a part of with two dozen attendees. Over time, the group kept losing members.

When the opportunity came to lead it, only three people were showing up for the discussions.

I didn't have the time or energy to take over, so I considered letting it die.

A couple of months later, I gave it a try to practice and share what I was learning.

I shared in the company's intranet what I was up to and invited people to participate.

In less than a year, the group had consistent attendance of 50 people or more.

As the audience grew, I gave people the opportunity to facilitate meetings, share their ideas, and lead the discussion.

Some started facilitating their own groups.

After I left the company, I invited a recurring participant to take over and he accepted the baton.

This group now hosts 300+ individuals looking for ways to lead their life.

The decision to host the group and confidently share what I was doing, is like a loud noise that catches the attention of the zombie herd.

Some of the walking dead get curious and break off the herd to figure out what's the noise.

The more they hear the noise, the farther away from the herd.

The conversation in the symposium functions as the human who then directs the curious in a specific direction.

During the process, while this is not how the walking dead universe works, I see the zombies waking up to the idea that they too can do something different.

The programming fades and their curiosity for more gains intensity.

What starts as a shiny object to create a new line becomes a catalyst for the individual to break away from the line altogether.

Our actions to claim our space can serve as an example to help others do the same without us having to convince them.

The Ultimate Negativity Cure: Be Like Water

"You must be shapeless, formless, like water.
When you pour water in a cup, it becomes the cup.
When you pour water in a bottle, it becomes the bottle.
When you pour water in a teapot, it becomes the teapot.
Water can drip and it can crash.
Become like water my friend."

~Bruce Lee

What did Bruce Lee mean and how is it related to the Greatness Within Framework and filtering criticism?

I see two characteristics: **adaptability and being.**

Adaptability: A natural thriving skill

Humans seem to be the only species that voluntarily lives in many climates. It's from extreme cold to extreme heat, there are humans not just living but thriving in the environment.

When we consider that humans aren't the strongest species, we are the dominant one because of our capacity to adapt and use our intellect to use our surroundings to survive and succeed.

"You must be shapeless" means, to me, that I must avoid thinking of my current understanding of myself and the world as

absolute. I must continuously challenge what I know, think, and do to keep improving and learn what's necessary to make my vision a reality.

Thus, when someone or our gremlins show up to ruin our parade, we can recognize our capacity to adapt to any scenario and understand that whatever it is said, it is not a death sentence or destruction of who we are and what we are trying to accomplish. It is just another vessel trying to contain us like a cup trying to hold the ocean.

Being: The Art of Showing Up
Water continues to be water regardless of the container.

Similarly, we can choose to be ourselves regardless of where we go and who we are talking to.

Sometimes the circumstances will temporarily stop us. Sometimes it will slow us down. And, sometimes it will make us stumble and crash.

But we can continue to be ourselves and find other ways to keep going.

Applying It to The Journey: Do What Clicks & Eliminate The Rest
I have hinted at this throughout the book so I won't go deep on this one.

The most productive way I have found to *"deal with life"* is to adapt to the situations while still being myself.

No matter who says something I make sure that it's in alignment with what I am trying to accomplish and who I want to be in this world.

What worked before may not work going forward. What didn't work then could work now.

What's important is that I continue to seek alignment.

If something strongly resonates with you, take it, test it, monitor results, and adjust if needed.

If something stopped helping you move forward, then consider letting it go.

Ultimately, you have the power to choose and no obligation to pay attention. As the title of this chapter says: **feedback is unavoidable, listening is optional.**

I'll talk to you in the next chapter to discuss step #5 of the framework, **gratefully welcome the journey.**

> *"Life is a grindstone; whether it grinds you down or polishes you up depends on what you're made of."*
>
> ~Jacob M. Braude

Chapter 17: The Secret Power of Gratitude

"Learn how to be happy with what you have while you pursue all that you want."

~Jim Rohn

You probably noticed that the entire book is a personal story sprinkled with a few insights distilled from experience and what I have studied without directly telling you what to do.

This is aligned with my purpose statement: *I believe we not only have the right to control our lives, we deserve to create them. Thus, I help individuals rediscover their capacity to create a life worthy of them...a life they love.*

It's not my place to tell you what to do because what works for me may not work for you, and I haven't lived your story.

I am sharing what I apply in life. I challenge, discover, claim, filter, and welcome.

This is the last step of the framework and the one I feel the least prepared to talk about but I am doing it anyway.

Throughout the book, I have been stressing the need to approach this as a process of discovery and avoid thinking of the right or wrong way to do it.

I have been doing it because I have enough observations that life doesn't follow a straight path.

My journey to where I am has not gone according to plan. I cannot recall a plan that has worked how I originally designed it.

Thus, I can approach this journey with a fixed mindset or a learner mindset. I have done both and, in this chapter, I present my case for picking the latter approach.

Fair warning, this chapter will probably sound woo-woo and philosophical. I propose to approach it with the willingness to ponder on the ideas and test them in your life.

Let's begin.

The Context

I recognize that no matter how much I plan and try to do it a certain way, the universe can change directions and not follow a straight line.

There are so many things outside my control that it's impossible, probably unnecessary, or wasted effort, to plan every detail and commit to a specific plan.

- Random people show up to help,
- Doors thought to be wide open are quickly shut, and,
- Challenges that look like obstacles, at first, become catalysts for success.

Additional to life's surprises, there seems to be a difference when we go through life with a sense of wonder and gratitude.

- Life appears to be easier to handle
- Obstacles become blessings
- Stress goes down and creativity goes up, and,
- A positive state of mind seems to attract other good things into our lives.

This chapter attempts to help you recognize the value of a positive state of mind and apply it so creativity can flow, challenges become learning moments, obstacles become another rung of the ladder and the stress of feeling forced to work hard and push through the storm vanishes.

This chapter is about having faith that things will align if we can operate from a place of discovery, learning, and gratitude for the opportunity to create.

I submit to you **six (6) concepts I have learned from gratefully welcoming the journey:**

1. Four Ways We Create Life
2. The Earner vs. The Steward
3. Anything Can Be A Door
4. The Dream Must Never Be At The Mercy of The Plan
5. Not Everyone Survives The Journey
6. Rent Only Goes Up and Never Ends

Concept #1 - Four Ways We Can Create Life

This is another idea I heard from my mentor Paul, and I have experienced its truth.

The concept speaks to the different ways I can engage with life.

1. Life happens to me
2. Life happens by me
3. Life happens because of me
4. Life happens through me.

I'd like to frame them as stages:

1. I have no choice
2. I see it but don't know what to do with it
3. I make it happen
4. I let it flow

I Have No Choice

We all know the phrase well and people who seem to live by it.

This is what the world describes as a victim mentality. The person is given a fixed set of cards and they have to play the game of life with it forever.

The *"I have no choice"* life is very stressful. It's being in constant survival mode.

I recall many instances in which I said I needed to quit my job because they didn't pay me enough to deal with the shit show.

Yet, I never did because I believed I had no choice but to stay in a job that was allowing me to stay in the United States and make good money.

I also couldn't quit because it meant I had 10 days to leave the country.

If you aren't familiar with how work visas function, the company I worked for had to sponsor my visa, and until I had a permanent resident's card, I couldn't quit.

If I quit, it meant I was forfeiting the option to have permanent residency and I needed to leave the country because I was no longer sponsored by the company.

Thus, I sucked it up and stayed the course for at least five more years.

I had the same mindset back when I was in college.

There's a night that comes to mind where I was chatting with a church friend. I was sharing how I felt out of place and I wasn't happy. With a direct approach he said, *"then come back home...you have been saying the same thing to me for a couple of years...come back."*

I didn't do it. My mom wanted me to get a college degree and learn English, so I stayed and finished.

What kind of life can it be if we believe that we have no choice as to what we do and we are forced to deal with life as is?

This is best known as the *victim mentality*.

I See It But Don't Know What To Do With It

> *"Better the known evil than unknown angel."*

In this stage, one learns the set of cards can be changed because we see that other people have done it.

We think about the possibility of making a change but we are uncertain on how to proceed. We don't feel *safe* rocking the boat.

We say things like

- I kind of have a good thing going here
- That's cool but I'm not that person

- I'm excited about doing this thing but...

This stage is frustrating because we can see there are options and the grass is greener somewhere else but we aren't sure how to make it happen so we choose the safety of what we already have.

It's what James Allen described in his book, *"As a Man Thinketh,"* **"People are anxious to improve their circumstances but are unwilling to improve themselves; they, therefore, remain bound."**

When I am in this mindset, I operate as a daydreamer.

I have dreams about greater things and see that life can be better. Now and then, I get lucky and good things come my way but I'm either not sure how to repeat those situations or I am unwilling to go figure out how to do it.

Thus, I keep going through the motions with just a little more positivity.

I Make It Happen

"When we choose to be responsible and creative rather than reactive, we stop being victims of our lives."

~Karen & Henry Kimsey-House

I consider this stage the outcome of taking action after we become aware there are options. I liken it to playing the hand dealt with the best of my abilities, or asking for a new hand, and intentionally finding a way to win.

It is the classic achiever mentality. It's taking control of what's happening, working hard, getting creative, and earning a place among the successful elite.

In this mindset, the life I have is a direct result of my commitment to solving problems and being resourceful.

I paid the price; therefore, I deserve it.

It feels good to be in this stage because it's a significant accomplishment and something most people avoid pursuing.

The main drawback I see is the weight that comes from taking all the responsibility to make it work because it's all about the *"self-made"* success story.

It is fueled by the belief that to take charge of life, sacrifices must be made, everything requires effort, and things must be kept under control.

When do we rest?

Life is good but seems to come at a great cost and responsibility.

I Let It Flow

Earlier, I shared the story about arriving at the Paraguayan Consulate with 50% of the materials needed and having to stay the entire day instead of the expected half day.

I also mentioned my promise to the host of returning the next day no matter what.

When I made the promise, I had no clue about how I would do it. I just went with it.

Rather than think about it and come up with a plan to do it, I went about the day's activities and stopped thinking about it.

Towards the end of the day, an idea came.

I remembered there was a line in a hallway near the coaches' pickup area for the hosts to request trainers.

Hence, I told the host he should show up tomorrow and request me as the trainer.

The next day came and rather than waiting, I waited by the pickup line. I also went around and recruited other coaches to come with me.

As soon as I saw the driver from the prior day, I walked to him and said we are ready.

The line's facilitator was too busy with other things to think about what was going on.

Thus, away we went.

A similar experience happened when I launched the Open to Anyone 3-day Leadership Summit.

I planned nothing. I went with the flow of things.

I remember having a script for my teaching sessions but I adapted to the room and let the words come out.

With 300 participants, including a handful that traveled from out of state, I'd call it a success even though it wasn't professionally planned.

These are a couple of examples of instances in which life can be very satisfying without extensive effort and a system to control everything.

There are instances in which I am present in the moment and calmed enough to be led by intuition.

It's life happening through me. It's a moment of flow. It's a period where everything seems effortless.

I call it *welcoming what life offers.*

How Do These Perspectives Relate To Creating A Life Worthy of You?

It all comes down to choosing.

It's choosing how we interpret what's happening around us and the role we play in the world.

Does that mean there's no hard work, planning, or strategy involved? No.

It means that the mindset we take, at any given time, makes it easier or harder to deal with the journey.

I can see life as a victim, a daydreamer, an achiever, or let it flow.

For the past three years, I have been trying to *"make it happen."*

Trying to build a business doing what I love.

I have...

- Hired mentors and coaches
- Invested thousands in different programs
- Tried four business models
- Worked through the night

- Attended over a hundred networking events
- Had hundreds of prospecting conversations
- Develop dozens of plans and strategies
- Created over 200 hours of content
- Answered hundreds of support questions
- And, many more things…

Yet, I'm not as far as I thought I would be.

Why?

Because in making it happen, I have been too stressed and desperate to be truly present when interacting with a potential client to serve them well.

The focus on getting stuff done has distracted me from finding my core message.

The progress has been like a shotgun blast instead of laser-focused sniper shot.

However, while assessing the prior years, most of my successes came from things I wasn't even trying to do.

- An impromptu tech support conversation with someone without thinking about making money ended with them offering to pay me for my time.
- A stranger hired me for a website refresh from reading one of my answers in a social media group.
- Random ideas that came to me in the middle of a program I was reviewing turned into a paid workshop where I helped a couple of dozen people with their business.

Essentially, 80% of the revenue generated came from things I didn't plan for. I was simply going about my day.

If I had to guess what made the difference between the hard work to produce 20% of return and the 80% coming from living life, I would say it was being open to welcoming life and living in the moment.

Like the Paraguay experience and the Leadership Summit, I didn't try to control things. I just went with it and permitted myself to adapt.

In relinquishing control, I relaxed enough to stay focused on serving the person in front of me. In return, the recipient of my service felt enough safety to trust me.

In my relaxed state, I remained calm and assertive. This allowed me to properly serve the individual and help them solve a problem. As a result, I was hired.

Throughout those interactions, I was working hard but it didn't feel like it. I was focused on serving the other person and enjoying the moment.

What made it possible was allowing life to flow through me rather than forcing it to happen.

As always, the choice is yours. As you go through your journey, work on allowing life to happen through you rather than always trying to control it.

Life is truly a reflection of what we allow ourselves to see.

~Trudy Symeonakis Vesotsky

Concept #2 - The Earner vs. The Steward

I see this as a personal philosophy more than something learned from someone.

What's The Earner Mindset?

For most of my life, I have thought success must be earned through effort and sacrifice. I had to pay my dues.

Yes, there is a requirement to put in the work but I'm not sure it must feel difficult to accomplish great things.

But I spent most of my life only valuing successes where I felt I put in a lot of energy and effort to get them.

I use the Leadership Summit as an example.

Even though it was a success story, the next day it was over, I simply moved on to the next thing.

I don't recall taking a moment to celebrate and welcome the praise several people were giving me. I checked the box and looked for something bigger to do.

I didn't think of it as a great accomplishment until I started writing this book.

Why?

Because the entire process felt easy and painless. Everything worked without putting in much sweat or mental equity. Hence, a low effort meant it was nothing to write home about.

I didn't think I earned the right to claim success.

I have repeated the behavior often throughout my life and it's probably the reason I have a hard time recalling accomplishments, asking for testimonials, and writing an awesome *curriculum vitae*.

Because of my belief that great things must come with a high level of sacrifice and hard work, I dismiss most of my successes as part of normal life and only remember the ones I had to persevere to achieve.

I call this way of engaging with life the **earner mindset.**

The earner believes:

- Everything must be earned through effort and sacrifice
- If compliments are given for things easy to do, that's just *"people being nice."*
- If success comes easy, it's not a cause for celebration
- Help from others is the last resort after hard work hasn't paid off in solving a problem

The main question the earner asks is: *what am I going to have to do or sacrifice to deserve X?*

As it is expected, there are different intensity levels of this mindset but it boils down to *"if you want it, you have to earn it".*

Alternatively, **one can engage with life from the perspective of a steward.**

What's The Steward Mindset?
A steward manages or looks after something considered valuable.

This person values what they are taking care of with a sense of respect and honor.

A steward...

- Is given the opportunity rather than something they directly *"earned"*
- Commits to the cause and does whatever is needed to manage the resources effectively
- Uses their talents to improve the brand and leave a legacy
- Works hard to spread the message
- Doesn't have to sacrifice
- Is grateful for the opportunity to serve

While my descriptions differ, I do see similarities when it comes to effort.

The key distinction comes from the impact of the mindset.

One person sees life from this place of equating value to the amount of effort put in. The other values what life brings and works hard to take advantage of the opportunity.

Both individuals will make it happen but they don't experience life the same way.

As an earner, I've had a stressful and unappreciated journey at times. Not because of lack of people thanking me for a job well done or unappreciative of my help, but because I was quick to dismiss their words and gratitude by comparing it to how much effort I put into it.

An interesting observation about this mindset is that sometimes I looked for ways to feel like I sacrificed something to help another person or achieve a goal. I looked for ways to make my work harder.

How messed up is that?

In contrast, shifting to being a steward of my talents and the opportunities life brings has changed how I perceive stress, engaging with people, and goals.

There's a sense of freedom that comes from not having to prove anything to anyone and not having to seek validation in what I do.

It's simpler to show up and value things based on how much I get to use my gifts, how aligned is the task with my purpose, and how much someone else is benefiting from what I am doing.

Does that mean hard work and trade-offs aren't needed? No.

It means I stopped expecting life to be hard to be of value and I interpret most things as an opportunity to take care of things.

I can see everything as a way to *earn my way up,* or I can see everything as an *opportunity to do what I do best because I am just taking care of what was given.*

Concept #3 - The Dream Must Never Be at The Mercy of The Plan

I am often guilty of doing it. It's part of my habit to do pros and cons analyses and figuring out everything before starting.

The phrase is another one from Paul as he teaches about goal setting.

It rings true because it's what I have done and what I see my clients do.

A common example of this concept is using past performance to determine what is a possible growth target for the following year.

We think because we have consistently had a 10% increase in the past, a reasonable goal should be 10% with a *"stretch"* goal of $15% to 20%.

But what if the economy changes or regulation is implemented that nullifies the past assumptions? What if a new technology comes up and changes the entire game?

Another example is when we determine that step seven will not work so we better go back and do some research before we begin the project.

I lost count of how often I have done it.

I have a love-hate relationship with project planning because I have had so many stressful experiences with a project manager adamant that everything needed to be accounted for in the project plan.

If something wasn't in the project plan, it would not get done.

The problem with it was that we were setting up project plans for a task that was going to start one year later.

How many things can change in one year? How likely is it that the plan would still be viable in 12 months?

Furthermore, using experience to plan a dream forces the mind to work under the constraints of what has happened before and the current knowledge.

It's like telling a kid to solve a 12th-grade problem with 7th-grade tools. That's very limiting.

I experience this when I do goal setting. I tend to look at my past and let prior results be the basis for the future.

The highest salary I have had is in the low six-figures income.

How comfortable do you think I feel when I write my goal to be the first one in my family to reach a 7-figure compensation?

What has worked so far is switching from setting the goal as something to obtain to set it to give room for creativity and to learn what is needed to make it happen.

The objective is to switch from "Can I do it?" to "What can I discover, learn and do to make it happen?"

> *"A dream is the seed of possibility planted in the soul of a human being, which calls him to pursue a unique path to the realization of his purpose."*
>
> *~Sharon Hull*

Concept #4 - Anything Can Be A Door

To me, it's like turning the radio to a specific station. For me to see the opportunity, I must be in the correct frequency.

I have mentioned this concept in prior chapters so I'll be brief.

There are two required beliefs in this statement:

1. I can see opportunity in every obstacle
2. Life works in mysterious ways.

I see both as part of gratefully welcoming the journey of creating a life worthy of us.

Opportunity in Every Obstacle

I consider this view as part of committing to being a learner on this journey. It's about using every situation as a way to learn more about myself, the world, and others.

Obstacles can show me how much I have grown, be a closed-door that gives space for something better or teach me something I will need later.

I have heard that life has a way of giving us the same experiences until we learn the lesson.

- Getting *kicked out* of a prior role opened the door for me to live with purpose.
- Getting *"fired"* from my *secure* job gave me time to heal emotional wounds, pursue my passion, and see my baby daughter grow.
- Someone asking me to take over the Leadership Symposium when I had no time or energy to do it, gave me a stage to test my newfound passions.
- Hosting a leadership summit with no budget, no team, and under the scrutiny of human resources, helped me see the power of inviting people on a journey and betting on myself.
- Interpersonal issues in high school helped me develop resilience to handle being on my own in a foreign country without freaking out.

So much goes on in life we cannot know what fruits can come from the things that happen to us.

At any point, we can choose to be engulfed by the circumstances of life or we can interpret it as another step along the path of our becoming.

The Mysterious Ways

Unfortunately, I have not kept track of how often the universe helps me make progress in unexpected ways.

As a believer, I subscribe to the idea that *"God works in mysterious ways."*

Nowadays, I think the mysterious ways are simply created by my lack of ability to see the bigger picture of my life.

> *"It's hard to see the picture when you are in the frame."*

With the leadership summit, a lady I didn't know contacted me and offered to project manage it for me. Another person offered to record and live stream the event.

The first time someone paid me for coaching was what I had wanted to be paid without me asking them.

Getting *"fired"* was something I kind of asked for. I remember the moment I strongly felt the need to leave the company and said so to myself. I didn't quit but two months later I was informed my position was being eliminated. This change of job situation gave me the space to focus on raising a family and identifying many lessons I shared in this book.

At the time of the event, I may have been flustered, angry, frustrated, surprised, or confused, but I simply didn't have the awareness of the entire picture.

I'm sure you have had similar *coincidences*.

Part of welcoming the journey is being open to the possibility that life may throw unexpected circumstances that can fast track your journey.

Concept #5 - Not Everyone Survives The Journey

"People are like dirt. They can either nourish you and help you grow as a person or they can stunt your growth and make you wilt and die."

~Plato

We have all heard the phrase attributed to Jim Rohn before, *"we are the average of the five people we spend the most time with."*

Whether that's true or not, it does seem to present a strong case.

Maybe you are like me and enjoy people watching.

Sometimes and sit and pay attention to groups of people and analyze who they are spending time with.

Almost every time, I notice a pattern in the thinking and personalities of the group.

In the workspace, they call it *"group think."*

I think it's more human nature. We connect with people similar to us.

I believe it is part of tribal ancestry and culture.

The blind spot is that it creates a closed system that, without new information, can end up outdated. It's like living in a bubble.

The bubble does not benefit what we are trying to accomplish. We cannot become a better version of ourselves by relying on current information available in our bubble.

This is why, in step #4, *Confidently Filtering Your Critics*, I proposed to partner with people committed to helping us and challenge us to keep improving.

If we take the need to feel connected and belong as the driver for this behavior, when a person reinvents themselves, their current circle of friends may not be a fit.

In reflection, I have seen it happen regularly.

- My high school friends are on their journey and our interests don't align. I still care for them but I am not comfortable sharing my dreams with them.
- Coworkers I talked to on and off work are now absent from my life.
- People I used to partner with to brainstorm ideas are no longer interested.
- Social groups I used to visit are no longer exciting.

As growth happens, people change and paths can go in different directions. It's part of the journey.

If I am to summarize it into a sentence I'd say, "Not everyone is meant to be in our lives forever. Some stay more than others but every single one of them plays their part along the way."

- Some do a pit stop to quickly share some wisdom or encourage us and then go on their merry way.
- Others are like tour guides that come alongside us for some time to teach us the ropes and then leave when we are ready.

- Several people are pacesetters who help us from afar by going before us and sharing their findings.
- A few are like soulmates who believe the same things and give us company and support all the way. And,
- Many provide a scenic view because they are not on the bus with us.

Endings are part of the story and the key is to discern when an ending is necessary and being okay with letting go.

"In everyone's life, at some time, our inner fire goes out. It is then burst into flame by an encounter with another human being. We should all be thankful for those people who rekindle the inner spirit."

~Albert Schweitzer

Concept #6 - Rent Only Goes Up and Never Ends

"Everything worthwhile is uphill. The purpose gives you the reason to go uphill. Your giftedness defines if you get uphill."

~John C. Maxwell

The Law of Trade-offs, in the 15 Invaluable Laws of Growth book by John C. Maxwell, states we must be willing to trade things of lesser value for things of greater value.

I used to think growth was like leveling up in a video game. I did some work, paid the price, and then moved on to the next level. But I was wrong.

Have you noticed that when you become aware of something, you can't erase it?

It can be a thought, a type of behavior, a scene, a habit, etc.

Once it is noticed, we can ignore it but we cannot forget it.

I see that in this journey we are on. If I want to keep moving towards my ideals, I cannot simply revert to old patterns, people, and things.

Furthermore, to the farther we go, the higher the level of commitment required.

It's like reaching an ideal body weight.

- Letting go of the first 20 pounds is achieved by moving more and changing portion sizes.
- Next is substitutions with better quality foods.
- Then, having the discipline to maintain compliance with the diet plan.
- All the while, the volume of exercise increases.
- The more weight freed, the harder it gets to keep lowering body weight.
- Once the ideal weight is achieved, all those habits cannot be removed. Otherwise, it all comes back.

There's a reason people say weight management is a lifestyle change, not a temporary exercise program and goal.

The same applies to going from following other people's advice to creating a life that represents who we are.

What got us here, won't get us there. *Why?* Because if it did, we would already have it.

I won't pretend to know the price you must invest in executing your vision but I can share one thing that has cost me the most to give up to make room for what I want.

This is a recent event and I admit sharing it to process it myself.

In late 2012, I had my epiphany and lived intentionally.

In late 2016, I went to a vision retreat where, for the first time, I allowed myself to write my vision.

Part of the vision was to change the leadership culture of my department.

By now you know that never happened. But the dream was still alive years after I was removed from the company.

How is that possible?

In the awakening of my passion for leadership and personal development, I felt a huge fervor for addressing the communication and leadership gaps in my department.

I had the trust of many people involved in the daily operations, I had direct exposure to the issues, and I felt capable of coming up with solutions.

This dream got stronger after I became a certified Leadership Coach, Speaker, and Trainer with the John Maxwell Team.

This membership gave me access to worldwide coaches that could help me with any corporate problem.

Whether it was lack of influence, skills, or misaligned visions, I got little traction with this dream.

The success of my leadership development journey came from outside my department.

One reason I didn't leave my department is that I felt a commitment to make things better. If I left, it meant I had given up on my dream and others. And, I couldn't take it.

Thus, for years I took full responsibility if a leadership idea wasn't adopted or listened to. I thought I just needed to get better at communication and negotiation.

When my tenure ended, I felt I left something unresolved. I felt like a failure.

It took me the entire year 2018 to process the emotional strain of not fulfilling that dream. And, it took another year to recognize that I was still trying to please people who were never aligned with my interests.

It took another 12 months to internalize that I was forcing myself to fit in a place I never belonged.

After three years of processing, I finally wrote myself a letter that can be summarized in a sentence: I have nothing to prove and I have nothing to validate because what I bring is valuable and expected by others.

Since that moment, the internal struggle has disappeared and positive momentum has evolved.

Life is not perfect but I have made room for what's next.

My commitment to a prior dream that would not be realized cost me three years of emotional stress and misfired business ideas.

And I have to regularly remind myself of the statement, *"I have nothing to prove and nothing to validate"* because I catch myself getting into self-judgment or making myself busy trying to prove to some fictional person I am working on my vision.

The cost may be physical, emotional, mental, or spiritual, but rest assured it will continue to grow the higher up you go.

As the Buddha stated, "**attachment is the root of all suffering.**"

Sometimes the fastest way forward is letting go of the dead weight we are trying to keep alive.

It's Decision Time

"Perhaps more people would move forward towards their dreams if they considered the cost of doing nothing as much as they consider the price of going after their dreams."

~Chris Rollins

I heard the comedian Steve Harvey share that had God told him all the steps he had to go through to get to where he is today, he would have not accepted the journey.

My mentor, John Maxwell, responds in a similar way when someone tells him they want to be just like him. John's response is *"would you like to do what I did to get here?"*

I consider this the end of my framework and the beginning of yours.

As mentioned throughout the book, take what you need and ignore the rest.

It's time to consider how willing are you to be humble enough not to take yourself too seriously and let the flow of life support your journey.

It requires being committed to the vision but flexible with the methods to get there.

Pick one place to start and permit yourself to explore. You may be surprised with what you find.

Chapter 18: Connecting The Dots

"While there is nothing wrong with working hard or
challenging ourselves to reach for the stars, when these
actions stem from misguided attempts to prove our worth
in an absence of self-acceptance, they will
always leave us wanting."

~Karen & Henry Kimsey-House, CoActive Leadership

After finishing the content, I figured it would be beneficial to give an executive summary of the entire framework.

Suppose you and I are meeting at your favorite social gathering place to have a heart-to-heart conversation about life in general.

With your favorite drink at hand and comfort food on the side table, I begin to share this life framework I call **GREATNESS WITHIN: Five Steps to Stop Seeking Validation and Create A Life Worthy of You.**

I start with...

Why I Came Up With This Framework?

For 30 years, I went through life listening to the advice of loved ones, experts, career advisers, friends, and successful individuals.

I took this advice to heart and followed it to the best of my ability.

It worked.

Life had its challenges but it was relatively comfortable and I had nothing to complain about.

I landed a well-compensated job, made friends, and was making a difference in the company I worked for.

But, at the same time, I couldn't shake the feeling that something was off. I never quite fit where I was.

Then, it all came crashing down.

I was kicked out of my role and felt like I had failed.

I questioned my worth and doubted myself.

I had followed the best advice but somehow still failed to maintain the success. I still felt out of place.

I felt like I was living someone else's life. A life driven by other people's expectations and suggestions.

Hence, I decided to try again, but this time, I would do it my way.

I thought, *"I could fail following other people's best and well-meaning advice, I might as well try it my way. If I fail, then I am back where I started. I have nothing to lose."*

This decision started a journey that led to the realization there are ways to mold life to what matters to me.

Also, I noticed that I wasn't the only one in such a situation. Many people along the way felt similarly.

Hence, I made it my mission to help others do the same.

Who Is This For?

Aside from myself, I wrote this for a specific person.

I will call her Sophia.

Sophia is a purpose-driven individual who dreams of becoming a confident creator of her life.

It's not just about a professional career or working for herself. **It's about trusting herself enough to create a life that fully represents her.**

It's about creating a life that fits her like a glove.

Currently, Sophia's **focus is on living with purpose.**

Ultimately, Sophia **wants to have a life she loves.**

Right this minute, Sophia would be **ecstatic if she could know where to begin.**

Unfortunately, Sophia still needs to figure out how to find the confidence to be herself.

She is frustrated by the fact that others in her life and the people **she listens to for advice continue to suggest paths that haven't fit with her.**

Since they also tell her that her ideas won't work, she follows the best practices and plays it safe.

The main question she is wrestling with before making a move is: *"How can I follow my path without knowing if it will work?"*

Sophia is also still **hung up on her not wanting to disappoint her family and friends.**

In living with purpose, **she is convinced that others just want her to stay the same and stop "daydreaming."**

When all is said and done, **Sophia just wants to have a life that fits her and do what she loves.**

The **Greatness Within Framework** is an offer to help Sophia find the confidence to trust herself and purposely create a life worthy of her without needing validation from others.

What Is The Framework?

At the time of my decision to live intentionally, I had the choice to go back to what I knew worked or venture into an unknown that could bring me a sense of joy and belonging.

Additionally, I recognized that the new path needed a version of a reset.

The decades of education about what are valuable professions, how to make life choices, and what are the best practices to achieve success got me a level of success that left me feeling out of place.

Hence, if I wanted to pursue creating a successful and joyful life, I had to determine what was worth keeping to be used on my journey.

I called this **Step #1 - Passionately Challenge Everything.**

It's a way to unlearn something to make room for new ideas.

After challenging everything, I had to identify what to keep and what to replace or eliminate.

Absent awareness, I used familiar tools like a purpose statement, a vision, values, and strengths as the measuring stick.

I called this **Step #2 - Courageously Discover Your Light.**

I used *"courageously"* because I didn't know what I would find about myself and what would be affected by my decisions. It took courage to spend time with myself and deal with my internal demons.

With the measuring stick identified, I started applying it to my life.

I had a frame of reference to assess what helped me advance towards my goal, what didn't, and what was optional.

I could now determine what steps I could use to chart my course.

I called this **Step #3 - Purposely Claim Your Space.**

As I aligned parts of my life and shifted focus, others shared their feedback, criticisms, advice, and so on.

I was also searching for new people to go for help and support.

The issue I ran into was that not everyone had positive things to say. And, when I am also fighting self-doubt, it's detrimental to the dream.

I had to come up with a way to filter who should I listen to.

I called this **Step #4 - Confidently Filter Your Critics.**

Finally, as the journey progressed, some of the best steps forward were unexpected.

Also, I accepted that life is constantly changing and that it's nearly impossible to control. I had to learn to be flexible and move with it while still staying the course.

I could adjust the sails but not control the wind.

This approach of allowing life to do its thing and treat every day as an opportunity to grow is what I called **Step #5 - Gratefully Welcome The Journey**.

Thus, the framework was formed:

1. Passionately Challenge Everything
2. Courageously Discover Your Light
3. Purposely Claim Your Space
4. Confidently Filter Your Critics.
5. Gratefully Welcome The Journey

The words are intentionally chosen.

The steps are to challenge, discover, claim, filter, and welcome.

The greatness within comes from being passionate, finding the courage to do it, purposely move, confidently adapt, and gratefully experience the moment.

The steps represent the expression of our will to the universe.

The adjectives are reminders to trust ourselves.

How To Apply It?

The beauty of the framework is that it functions as a foundation rather than rules of engagement.

It is meant to help the person start their race and figure out how to run it.

If I am to suggest an approach it would be to quickly read through it without trying to agree or disagree with it. Instead, it is to get the structure and the tools shared.

With the bigger picture in mind, then pick one thing in the framework to test in your life and let the outcomes of the journey determine what's next.

The steps apply regardless of the method.

To be a confident creator of your life a benchmark is needed to assess what is applied and what isn't.

Finally, since very few things in life can be controlled, you must give yourself grace because things won't go as planned.

The latter is why I pushed often to approach this journey with a sense of learning and discovery.

What's Next?

Many things can be done after going through the book.

I'd love to have a conversation with you about what you are going through, what you gained from the book, and how I can help you on your journey.

Just email hello@juanononecoaching.com to keep the conversation going.

If that's too forward but you still want to do something meaningful with the book's ideas, invite one person you know who can benefit from the book to read it and discuss it with you.

If you haven't read the book and just skipped to this chapter, maybe the next step is to put the book to the test.

Ultimately, the choice is yours.

I thank you for your interest, your time, and your willingness to engage with me in this indirect form.

In peace,

~Juan
Beacon of Clarity and Confidence

Made in the USA
Columbia, SC
24 May 2021

37990777R00145